Alain Liebaert

MASTERING DECLINE

Stories *and* Lessons
From a Company
Making Profit
Against the Odds

Published by
LID Publishing
An imprint of LID Business Media Ltd.
The Record Hall, Studio 304,
16-16a Baldwins Gardens,
London EC1N 7RJ, UK

info@lidpublishing.com
www.lidpublishing.com

A member of:

businesspublishersroundtable.com

© Alain Liebaert, 2022
© LID Business Media Limited, 2022

Printed by Gutenberg Press, Malta

ISBN: 978-1-911671-60-2
ISBN: 978-1-911671-61-9 (ebook)

Cover and page design: Caroline Li

Alain Liebaert

MASTERING DECLINE

Stories *and* Lessons
From a Company
Making Profit
Against the Odds

MADRID | MEXICO CITY | LONDON
NEW YORK | BUENOS AIRES
BOGOTA | SHANGHAI | NEW DELHI

*"Our greatest glory is, not in never falling,
but in rising every time we fall."*

Oliver Goldsmith

CONTENTS

INTRODUCTION

Over the years, my family and friends have urged me to write down my experiences as a business-man: namely, how I succeeded in efficiently managing my family life *and* personal development while maximizing the profits of my declining company.

Unsurprisingly, as decline isn't the most glamorous of topics in business, it is a subject on which very little is written. While there are plenty of books about crisis in companies or public affairs, there are very few about how to manage decline over several years. It's the difference between a 'finite' game and an 'infinite' game. In the finite game, where the crisis passes over time, the aim is to simply win, whereas players of the infinite game do so for the sake of playing endlessly.

This infinite game, which I have been playing since the beginning of the 21st century, is a totally different ballgame from the one most current CEOs are suited to playing: one oriented around growth and short-term profits. But, given the speed at which times are changing, many of us might just end up playing the infinite game for far longer than we can imagine.

What are the characteristics of decline?
- Declining sales with no hope of recovery in the short or medium term
- Products that become too expensive to fulfil customers' expectations
- Production costs (personnel, energy, ecology, raw materials, etc.) that are not competitive with those of other countries

And what are the consequences?
- Declining profitability
- More debt
- Higher inventory
- Low morale and difficulty keeping key people in the organization
- A CEO fighting to find the necessary motivation to go on

This list could go on forever as decline has many faces, some more daunting than others.

This book is about how we at Liebaert Textiles, as a family and management team, managed to control decline and turn it to our advantage. It is meant to help long-established companies survive in declining markets. Its purpose is to share our experiences, give advice and help people in these difficult circumstances.

I am very critical of many institutions, but this is because of what I have experienced personally over 30 years. A lot of people will have different experiences and contrasting opinions and will therefore disagree with what I say. I am absolutely okay with that, provided they also respect my views on the matter.

I have been fortunate enough to be surrounded by an exceptional team, both at home and at work. My wife, Michou, has always been on hand to provide the very best advice, as have my four children since they were very young. Their dedication and their many insights over the past three decades have been invaluable in the various successes I've achieved in my life.

They've challenged me and they've not accepted dictatorship, while always remaining respectful, loving and caring. And I've always appreciated their honesty!

Being cared for by such intelligent, dedicated, loving and extremely efficient people has allowed me to maximize my efficiency. I work an eight-hour day, on average, and take 12 weeks of holidays every year with my family. That's quite unheard of for the CEO of a multimillion-euro business.

Being prudent with my time has also given me space for my life's great passion and joy: flying. At 42, I gained the airline transport pilot license (ATPL), having studied and trained in my free time for three years. I had to divide my dedication, attention and concentration between the flying courses, my declining company, my extraordinary kids, and my smart and beautiful wife.

Captain Liebaert in the cockpit: the best training and one of my many passions.

Having various commitments meant I needed to become an expert in time management. Thirty years later, this probably remains my biggest achievement. Being able to travel, fly and do lots of sports, mostly with my family, has allowed me to find the delicate balance needed to cope with the heavy burden of a declining company, without succumbing to the tunnel vision that infects most workaholics.

"*Do not let making a living prevent you from making a life.*"

– John Wooden

As a pilot, I also learned to be ever ready for the worst-case scenario, to accept my own limitations and to cultivate the skills expected of me in my position. Without those lessons, my business life would have unknowingly suffered.

Coupled with these helpful experiences as a pilot, my strong interest in geopolitical history has also been of huge use in my business career. Through reading and travelling widely, I have developed a genuine understanding and respect for other cultures and religions. This is evidenced in our tourism enterprise in South Africa, which has furnished me with a more tolerant approach to other cultures, while also teaching me the pros and cons of a partnership.

These axes of partnership, understanding and tolerance are central to the 'new economy,' a concept developed by my close friend Professor Michel 'Mike' de Kemmeter. Along with hundreds of leaders, experts and economists, Mike has been looking at a future where businesses and industries value more than the purely 'material' and 'tangible.' Instead, the new economy attempts to imitate the interconnectedness of nature, where all parts effectively communicate with each other. In this future, all stakeholders are equally considered, everyone is motivated by a clear purpose and no one is wasted. The new economy is a holistic system that will hopefully replace the broken business models we've been struggling with for so long.

My contribution here is designed as a companion piece to his. The hard reality of my story lends the necessary realism to his dream of a perfect, sustainable world.

Mike is just one of the many exceptional people I've met over the years. In their own way, each one has helped my development, through their successes as well as their mistakes and flaws. I will dedicate a section to them, their experiences and what lessons we can learn from these stories. They will, of course, remain anonymous. These are the fine people who taught me that one of the most difficult achievements in life is to be exceptional both in business and personally.

In no way have I achieved this goal: if I had to rate myself, I would say that I have been a good father, a decent husband, a fair boss and a rather difficult person. At the most I deserve a passing grade. But at least I know it and am working on improvements.

Always on the lookout for what might go wrong.

Part 1

LIEBAERT

HISTORY OF THE FAMILY AND FACTORY

Before entering into my advice about managing a declining family business, it is necessary
to put things in historical perspective and go
back in time a little bit – through five generations, two world wars and one chronic bout of
ongoing decline.

By going back to the beginning, we can follow
the long, prosperous but beleaguered legacy of
my family's company. This will give context for
the many staggering efforts we've made to save it
from decline since the start of the 21st century –
when mass production moved to the East and we,
in the West, were left with the rubble.

THE LION AND THE LILY

My family comes from Dikkebus, a small village near Ypres in West Flanders. Our name, Liebaert, derives from *luypaerdt*, a word referring to the lion on the Flanders county flag in the Middle Ages.

During the Hundred Years' War, between France and England, the Flemish cities often sided with England, defying their lord and master, the king of France. The Liebaerts, later also known as the Klauwaerts, fought against the Leliaerts, a name derived from the word for 'lily.' These people were allies of the French, symbolized by the lily, which could be found on the French king's flag.

DEINZE

The Liebaerts have always been notable and important citizens in their city. They were lawyers, notaries, judges and later, most importantly of course, beer brewers. Gustave, son of the beer brewer Jean, married Eliza Van Heuverswijn from Deinze and left Dikkebus and settled in Deinze around 1860 as the small city's doctor. He was actively involved in local politics as a Liberal Party municipal representative and contributed to the cultural development of the region.

His eldest son, Alfred, was also a doctor. Alfred emigrated to South Africa to join the Boers in their struggle against the British, acting as head of the Belgian Ambulance Division. He led an adventurous life in Africa, marrying a circus dancer, with whom he travelled across the region founding hospitals. As a small boy, my room was decorated with Zulu weapons and artefacts from Alfred's travels.

Alfred's son, Jean, volunteered in the Belgian army at the start of the First World War and was sadly killed in the First Battle of Ypres in 1914. Out of sorrow, Alfred put his uniform on again to fight the Germans alongside his old enemies, the Brits, in Namibia. Another crazy twist in our family history.

THE MILL BEGINS

It was Alfred's younger brother, Marcel, who, at the tender age of 17, started the textile company with Octaaf Goeminne, another young man from Deinze. Octaaf was the senior of the two at 23 years old. They started in 1887 with manual narrow weaving machines, producing belts, braces, women's suspenders and other accessories. It wasn't long before the hand-operated machines were replaced by modern ones powered by steam. Marcel and Octaaf also gained the ability to weave elastic ribbons with rubber.

Octaaf died very young and Marcel took over his part of the company from Octaaf's widow, whom Marcel supported both morally and financially for the rest of her life. This is how things were done in those days!

Marcel Liebaert celebrating the 50th birthday of his beloved company.

ON EITHER SIDE OF THE LINES

Marcel's son, my grandfather Henri, joined the fight against the Germans on the Yser Front (in Belgium) during the First World War. Having studied in the German town of Krefeld, he could speak the language fluently. This ability afforded him the privilege of a very risky responsibility. Henri went out into no man's land, in front of the Belgian lines, listening to what the troops in the German trenches were saying to each other. Only 30 miles away, his father, Marcel, was working back in Deinze – territory occupied by Germany.

Father and son didn't see each other again until Belgium was liberated four years later.

Marcel was also spying on the Germans, an enterprise that eventually led to his capture and a year's incarceration. But that was a soft mercy. His best friend, another spy in the same cell, was executed. Miraculously, the German court couldn't prove Marcel was involved.

Henri Liebaert on the Yser Front in 1916.

Henri and Robert: the second generation, 1919.

He was released to the ruins of post-war Belgium. Being right beside Deinze station, his company was destroyed by the Allies' shells when they liberated Belgium. But he was finally reunited with his son, who returned home a war hero to help his father rebuild the factory from scratch along with his younger brother, Robert.

TAKING PUBLIC OFFICE

After rebuilding the business, Henri turned his attention to other offices. He entered politics, becoming a very successful Liberal politician, including as the Belgian Minister of Finance. Subsequently, he became the governor of the World Bank for Belgium and president of the Liberal Party. Later, after his business had survived *another* world war, he played an important role in the *Koningskwestie*. Known as the 'Royal Question' in English, this major political crisis determined his beloved country's survival as a kingdom. Without politicians like my grandfather, Belgium could have been committed to the mists of time. Eventually, following a decorated career, he quit politics in 1959. It was time to go back to the mill, which his son (my father, Andre) and nephew (Jean) had just joined, marking the third generation of our family enterprise.

They built a second factory, producing warp-knitted elastic fabrics, and we were one of the first factories to use Lycra™ in our fabrics. We are also the oldest one remaining in business – that is a certainty!

Warp knit machine, Ernst Saupe, 1936: one of the first warp knit machines ever built.

THE THIRD GENERATION

The tenure of Andre and Jean, during the 1970s and 1980s, saw a lot of turbulence. There were currency devaluations of the French franc, the Italian lira and the British pound, which hampered the company's competitiveness as all of our competition then were European companies. The Cold War and the oil crisis after the Yom Kippur War didn't do us any good either. Sales went up and down, and we were stuck with commodity products; everybody was making the same products and fighting over price because there was no creativity or differentiation.

At the end of the 1970s, Henri and Robert both died. The burden of business landed on my father, Andre. A highly intelligent and driven man, he spread his wings wide, taking Liebaert international, with offices in Paris, London, New York and Stuttgart. His gift was for product, while being very creative and an excellent salesman too. He was a charismatic leader, an exceptional father and a textile visionary. Under his leadership, Liebaert became the undisputed world leader in high-end elastic fabrics. He alone did more for our expansion, image and techniques than the two generations before combined.

DEDICATION FOLLOWS DEVASTATION

Tragically, my father died from cancer at the age of 55, only a couple of years after I had entered the company in the late 1980s. I was handed the daunting task of succeeding an exceptional man.

Alain and his father André: forever best friends.

Prior to the 1990s, the company hadn't been very profitable. The second and third generations had lost a lot of money and energy fighting each other – looking for compromises instead of running the company. It had been run by two branches of the same family – my dad's partner was his cousin – making Liebaert a two-headed monster. This bicephalic management system only bred jealousy, greed and mistrust. What value greed did bring was always cancelled out by the larger shadows of the other two factors. A recipe for disaster!

TWO HEADS HURT BUSINESS

This structure also damaged our finances. Sharing the company's commercial organization, as well as its management, generated two competing commercial policies in the company – a total mess. My father fought relentlessly to achieve results while his own partner was doing the exact opposite. Day after day, they were head to head. This frequent fighting ate up valuable energy needed to secure the company's future and keep up with our competition. French, German and Austrian narrow weavers were rapidly expanding while our company was caught up in quibbles and conflict. The opportunity to become the biggest elastic knitter and narrow weaver in Europe was lost.

I could write a whole other book about the dark side of our family business, but I'd imagine it would be quite tedious and of no interest to anyone else, especially because many family businesses have been confronted with much worse scenarios.

Whether the business has one head or two, and whether it's a family business or otherwise, textiles – especially at the high end – has always been a worrisome sector of the economy. Many fashionable producers with a lot of know-how did very well until the new century began. But then the tide changed rapidly and the textile business as we knew it ceased to exist.

MY ARRIVAL

I entered the company in 1989, having gained a master's degree in applied economics from the University of Antwerp. Before that I worked for a couple of years as a management consultant, reorganizing companies on a 'no cure, no pay' basis – the only way to work with consultants in my view.

Our narrows company had been making huge losses for a decade and my expertise was needed to turn it around. I told the older generation that I would either save or close this narrows factory – our original product! It was making €4 million in turnover in an industry worth €25 million, and it was losing more than €1 million. I saw no reason beyond sentiment to keep open a factory that had been making losses for more than ten years.

My father agreed but only on one condition: that we would respect and protect our loyal workforce and avoid a social bloodbath. I followed his wise and humane instructions, for he was my role model as a boss.

FINANCIAL TRIAGE

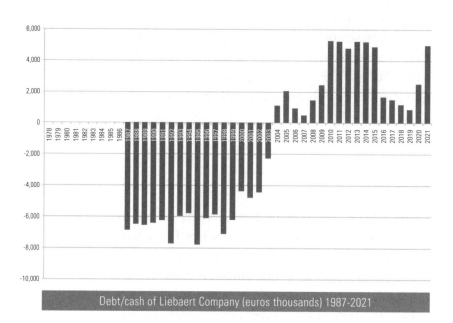

Debt/cash of Liebaert Company (euros thousands) 1987-2021

Revenue and cash flow of Liebaert Company (euros millions) 1987-2021

Within my first three years at the narrows mill, I managed to stop the bleeding and create positive cash flow. I cut costs, stopped making 'on call inventory' (inventory we kept for a certain period for one customer with a promise that they will eventually buy the product; unfortunately, they often changed their minds and didn't keep their word and we were stuck with worthless products) and no longer sold to loss-making customers. Over half of our sales had been made below cost! While sales dropped by 25%, our EBITDA (earnings before interest, taxes, depreciation and amortization) became positive again.

It was time to build some solid foundations from the ground up – the best way to build real sustainability into a company. We started by developing sales with *profitable* customers. Within five years both sides of our company – fabrics and narrows – were as profitable as each other. We'd corrected a major imbalance in our outfit.

Where it all happens: the Liebaert HQ today.

When my father died, management backed me to convince his cousin that I should manage the whole company myself. After four generations of disputes, the company could finally be managed by one person.

Watching my father – also my best friend – die from cancer each day for a year was a torture that I would not wish on my worst enemy. But through grit, will power and dedication, I've been able to maximize what he started.

I was a boss at the age of 28, missed my father dearly and had to fight against ageing managers, suppliers and customers who were convinced I was too much of a lightweight for the job. Being a boss is a very lonely job, but I experienced it far younger than most CEOs. It forged my character, my determination and my resilience. Unfortunately, though, it didn't make a better or a happier person out of me. It loaded me with worries, burdens and conflicts that a 28-year-old shouldn't have.

I only succeeded in my task thanks to the unconditional support of my wife, Michou, who for 30 years now has been listening to my worries, sometimes into the early hours, and has always given useful advice on options and strategies.

The fact that I had been a trainee at Liebaert Textiles for ten years from the age of 15 brought me an incredible amount of knowledge and experience that helped me both as a consultant and as a young boss. I was trained by my father and his team in production, finances, costing, sales, marketing, HR and IT, and travelled extensively to customers and suppliers.

My father even taught me how to negotiate with unions, the mighty actors of business life in Belgium.

This experience saved the day when I was on my own. And, in 1999 my second cousin, Pierre, entered the company to lead our IT department and our narrows mill.

Within a few years, I was able to build an exceptional team that lightened the burden of my loneliness. This team has evolved to almost completely control the company. Daniel (past COO), Kevin (COO), Greet (CSO), Luc (CFO), Philippe (research and development) and my son Mathieu (innovation) are all worth their weight in gold in my company and in my life.

You can never win a war on your own – you will always be stronger if you are surrounded by loyal managers, friends and family. I have won many battles and negotiations because my very capable and fierce opponents were fighting alone.

Michou and me with our children: our biggest achievement and greatest pride.

MIGRATION TO CHINA AND EUROPEAN DECLINE

SUMMONED TO LONDON

Textiles was rapidly approaching a hairpin turning point at the start of the 21st century.

Most mass-producing textile companies were based in the United States. One of them in particular was a top global brand – everyone was desperate to work with them. The volume of their production was enormous, and they most definitely had the best image, with their models and appealing marketing.

While their marketing techniques are perhaps questionable today, they were well above everyone

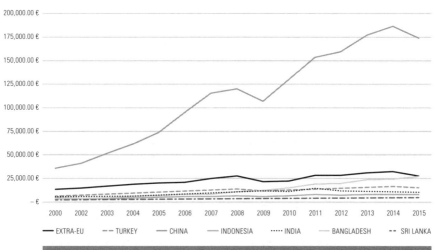

Export Evolution Clothing (Million EUR)

Clothing exports (euros millions) 2000-2015

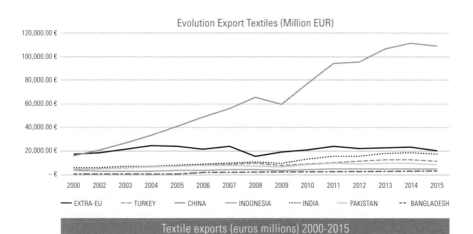

Evolution Export Textiles (Million EUR)

Textile exports (euros millions) 2000-2015

else in terms of marketing at the time. Everyone was looking to them for cues, even a traditional British household name that was *the* standard for quality mass production in Europe. I say 'Europe' because they had stores all over the continent back then. They don't now – most of those stores have closed.

But once upon a time this British company was the landmark for textiles, especially underwear, across Europe. They had 30–35% of the whole underwear market in the UK!

We were very big suppliers to them and we had a good relationship with them. They were loyal to us, unlike the top American brand, which we felt was just working with us for our novelty.

One day, the American empire made its big demand. All of its main European suppliers were summoned to a meeting in London. *Summoned*. We had to go. The illusion of it being an invitation was tissue thin.

So, from all over Europe we trekked. The company's vice president of purchasing, or merchandising, or something like that – who cares? – welcomed us from our travels by saying we were just chickens on a highway. A big truck with 'CHINA' written on the side was roaring toward us and we were all *going to die*.

What a welcome that was. You're going to die – great. But then this charming forewarning quickly evolved into something more immediate: actually, *you're dead* but you don't even know it yet.

I've never been bullied by *anybody*. I remained calm, thinking this showed a complete lack of class and education – to invite your suppliers to London only to be blunt, boorish and abusive to them. Well, we weren't going to be a supplier of theirs for much longer, I was quite convinced of that.

I thought, "Hey, I'm a chicken who can *fly!*" The truck will pass by me and hit a wall, just as I swoop over it. I had very little to lose. So, I said, "Thank you very much, but I'm not going to visit you any more – I'm not going to show you my range any more." They were completely shocked.

How did anyone dare speak to the mass-production fast-fashion goliaths like that? Well, I did dare. And here's exactly what I said in my letter:

Dear ————

First of all, I would like to wish you a happy and successful 2011.

We had a visit from your designers at the show in Paris and they sampled, as usual, a wide selection of fabrics.

I have the utmost respect for your company, especially for the marketing strategy and store set up.

Unfortunately, the relationship with Liebaert has always been a one-way street with us giving all our ideas away and getting nothing in return.

Your Asian vendors consider Liebaert much too expensive and will do everything in their power to source locally.

We have had many visits from your managers, including ————, and have invited a lot of your employees and vendors to our yearly three-day seminar in Belgium.

We even invested over $200,000 ten years ago to have our lab accredited by you. This shows you how committed we were.

All those efforts have been made in vain.

Liebaert was elected fabric designer of the year by Interfilière, and our company has never been as strong as it is now, with a growth of 25% last year.

We are more than ever seen as the most innovative fabric supplier in the world with exclusive machines, yarns and designs.

We invest €3 million every year to stay ahead of our Asian competition; nobody else in Europe makes such a commitment any more.

We had a very small programme with you five years ago, but I do not sense any commitment to grow the business with us.

We need to be two to tango and unless the senior management of your company makes a clear commitment to work with us, I do not sense any added value in continuing to show our ranges and send samples.

I say this without hard feelings but with a lot of regrets because I really think we could bring something unique to you.

I wish all the best to your company for the years to come.

Best regards,
Alain Liebaert

And that was that: goodbye big American brand. Never mind.

COURTING MORE TROUBLE

But it wasn't just them. A few years before, I'd had the same discussion with one of the garment producers of the UK customer I mentioned above. They were one of our main customers, with 10–15 factories around the UK and Ireland. They sent a letter on a Friday to all of their fabric providers, saying that from the Monday onwards they were going to pay all of their invoices with a 7% discount. They thought they were strong enough to impose a bullish strategy on us and that we'd have to take it.

But *no*. That same day I emailed all of their factories we were supplying at the time. I told them I also had some news about Monday: from then onwards, I wouldn't be supplying *any* of their factories worldwide with *anything*.

I don't believe in ultimatums. It's a tactic that will never end. If you give in once, they've got you. And, if you survive an ultimatum, you're dead without knowing it yet. It means you have a product that nobody will want unless you keep lowering your price.

Then the same thing happened with another one of our biggest customers. They represented 25% of our turnover and they said to us, "If you don't relocate to China, we won't buy from you." So, I had to bid them farewell, too.

HOMEWORK FROM EAST ASIA

We took a trip to China, Sri Lanka and Thailand and did a study, because our customers were trying to force us to have factories over there. Our study was very thorough and serious. We attempted to establish where would be the best and most affordable place to have a factory, as well as where we could find reliable and loyal customers.

Because if we were going to go over there – which would be a huge move and commitment – we wanted to be 100% certain that our customers would stay with us.

We did our homework. We studied Asia for two years, visiting our competitors. But it became resolutely clear to us that we couldn't transplant our Belgium-based business model there successfully. Our model is dependent on people and creative talent, not just on machines and finances. Even on the technical side, this requires a lot of training – people need to be taught to understand and operate the machines. We simply were not confident of finding the right people to make our operation successful in Asia.

The big American and European mass-producing fast-fashion goliaths all started with good ideas and genuine beliefs, but they threw them away for margins and mark-ups. I don't know of one big group that really delivers quality goods to their customers today. Not one. I'm talking purely about textiles of course. Other industries (such as technology or automotive) might be very different, but all of the big textile groups – all of them – have sold their souls to low-cost production.

One of my textile colleagues in Belgium owned the biggest weaving company in Europe in the 1990s. He employed close to 1,000 people and owned 3,000 weaving machines over several factories. His company delivered linings and sportswear fabrics to all the big brands.

One day he called me and said, "Alain, the Koreans have entered the market and I have lost most of my customers in six months. They sell at 25 euro cents a metre and my price is 75 cents; I cannot even buy the yarn for that price!"

Soon enough we were confronted with the same challenge: first our Italian and Spanish competitors started to sell elastic fabrics at €6 per metre, which was our cost price. Then the Chinese knitters came into the market at €3 per metre, forcing the Italians to go down to €4.5 per metre. This kind of diabolical spiral only ends with everyone losing.

Hourly Rate Textile Worker

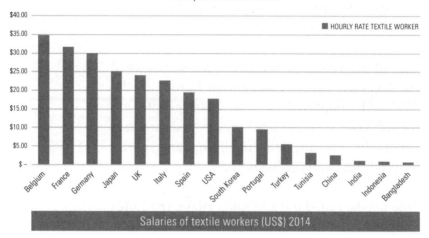

Salaries of textile workers (US$) 2014

We decided not to fight a battle that was already lost. We maintained our strategy of making high-end elastic fabrics, which we have done to this day with varying degrees of success.

So what remains in Europe is minimal. In Belgium, for example, in 1949 there were 1,000 factories and 180,000 people working in textiles. Of those 1,000 factories, there are five left, and there are now only 18,000 people working in the industry – ten times fewer, meaning that the industry has literally been decimated.

Employment in Belgian Textile Industry 1973-2016

The garment industry is the same. In 1949 there were 80,000 people working in the garment industry, whereas now there are about 7,000 left – down 90% in two generations. The UK mirrors this pattern too. In the 1990s, M&S had 30,000 people working in underwear alone and hundreds of garment-making suppliers. Now, about 90% of the garment industry in the UK has also disappeared.

Another problem is that there is not enough of a garment industry and there are not enough customers left in Europe to produce something economically viable. The market has become too small.

But, nonetheless, we will battle on. Why not try? Defeat is too easy and what we're losing is too important. We must protect some key industries.

Thankfully the COVID-19 crisis has brought some new insights that support our strategy and has helped us to establish a stronger local supply base.

TAPPED OUT OF TALENT

Another challenge that the textiles and garment industry in Europe is facing is a mass exodus of talent – a great migration – to Asia. This has led to almost all the textile schools shutting down.

There was no interest among potential workers in gaining knowledge of textile production – there was no point as it was a dying industry. Wages were very low, and everyone was fighting for survival. As a result, now that things are changing bit by bit and we are returning to a more local system of sourcing, we cannot find workers in textiles or garment-making.

This will be an even bigger challenge than the lack of raw materials in the future.

Liebaert factory workers, 1937.

THERE'S NO PLACE LIKE HOME

Yet, despite these concerns about the future, we remain serene. We've lost a lot of business – M&S, for example – but we've succeeded in finding new sources. Perhaps not such big customers. But it doesn't always have to be big.

We're happy with our core customers: they are loyal to us, they pay reasonable prices and they promise us continuous business.

As a team, we've always kept the same approach, the same resolve and belief. All our noses were pointed in the same direction regarding China and relocation. So we stayed in Belgium. As Greet Flement, our CSO, once commented: "We are extremely happy that we did not follow our competitors in doing what the customers were forcing us to do. Because we see what we see now. Most of our competitors who went over there came back or went bankrupt."

NUMBERS THROUGH THE DECADES

To really understand our story, you've got to look at the numbers. They don't lie. In one generation, we lost 60% of sales and trimmed the company down from 300 to 150 people without raising discontent among our workers. We dropped €7 million in debt, our equity has ballooned, and we have cash on hand.

1980S: GROWTH WITHOUT PROFIT

- **Turnover**: from €20 million to €25 million
- **Cash flow**: 3.8%
- **Investments**: 5% of turnover
- **Stock rotation**: from 2.5 to 3
- **Debt**: €7 million
- **1990s**: interest 8%
- **Equity**: €4 million
- **Customer credit**: 80 days
- **Personnel**: 300

1990S: GROWTH WITH PROFIT

- **Turnover**: from €25 million to €45 million
- **Cash flow**: from 3.8% to 23%
- **Investments**: 10% of turnover
- **Stock rotation**: from 3 to 5
- **Debt**: down from €7 million to €5 million
- **Equity**: from €4 million to €12 million
- **Customer credit**: down from 80 to 55 days
- **Personnel**: 300

2000–2021: DECLINE WITH PROFIT

- **Turnover**: down from €45 million to €16 million
- **Cash flow**: from 23% to 25%
- **Investments**: 8% of turnover
- **Stock rotation**: 5
- **Debt**: down from €5 million to €0 million
- **Equity**: from €12 million to €15 million
- **Cash**: €5 million
- **Personnel**: down to 150

TIMELINE OF DECLINE

The new decade, century and millennium arrived and a lot began to change for us. The best way to see our decline in size is year by year:

2003:

- We lose M&S as a customer (20% of our turnover) after we refuse to open a factory in Asia. Liebaert UK ceases operations as we close our Nottingham and London offices.

- Our sales to Triumph drop drastically
  after they also head for Asia. Liebaert
  Deutschland ceases operations as we close
  our Stuttgart office.

2008:

- We lose Chantelle (15% of our turnover) for
  the same reason as M&S and Triumph.
- Most US lingerie companies move to East Asia.
  Liebaert USA ceases operations as we close our
  New York office.
- We gradually and naturally reduce the number
  of our personnel from 300 to 230, without
  having to restructure.

2010–2014:

- The lingerie market continues to collapse as
  consumers opt to spend more on electronics
  and travel. This is compounded by big US and
  European brands' cheap products, made in
  Asia for mass-market consumption.
- We lose Lejaby (another 20% of our turnover)
  – a high-end lingerie brand that collapses from
  bad management.
- We make two small adaptations to our
  structure and cut costs. Our personnel level
  reaches a new low of 150.
- The social climate remains very positive
  as we have built a lot of trust with the
  unions over the years (a prerequisite for
  healthy restructuring).

2014:

- We combine our two factories (narrow weaving and fabric knitting) into one, optimizing both our resources and our personnel. This is essential for our subsequent structural changes.
- The old buildings sell at a very good price.

2015–2020:

- Hanes buys DIM and moves everything to Asia, losing us another 15% of our turnover. Liebaert France ceases operations as we close our Paris office.
- In 2018, the income from selling our old buildings in 2014 funds a brand new factory next to the existing knitting plant. This factory remains empty – either it will accommodate new projects or we will sell if the company needs cash. It is a good bit of insurance to have. Without a doubt, it is a major positive in a declining market.
- The fifth generation takes on the challenge as two of my children join the company. Together with their brother Emmanuel (our digital marketing guru), Mathieu and Camille put fresh, new wind in our sails. They have a native understanding of social media and digital marketing, while showing a youthful genius for branding.
- This new blood could be our salvation.

2020:

- Coronavirus paralyses the world and desperate measures are needed. The mayor of Deinze approaches us to produce face masks. That and drastic cost control save the day.
- We launch our new athleisure brand, RectoVerso™, and my daughter Camille becomes a brand manager of this new venture.
- Turnover drops from €17 million to €16 million, but cash flow remains at 20% and debt at zero. We have €2 million in cash, which should be enough of a buffer to deal with the strange and different future that is unfurling before us.
- Mathieu launches RV-Elite™, a revolutionary compression legging that enhances the performance of elite athletes. Five years of research with the Sport Science Laboratory – Jacques Rogge at Ghent University comes to fruition.

2021:

- With the combined help of our management team and the strong persuasive and negotiating skills of my son Mathieu, we are able to buy out the other part of the family. Finally, after a century of strife, we're in calm waters again. The future is bright and the horizon is far clearer.
- My wife Michou, my wisest and most trusted adviser since the beginning, becomes chair of the company.

As you can see, all the international expansion painstakingly pursued by my father was lost. The business contracted back to Belgium as we saw customer after customer depart and office after office close. Markets changed, tastes changed, but – while shifting in size – Liebaert held firm to its ethos and philosophy, with which we've so far survived decline with a revitalized future ahead. As Greet says: "Our company is not about making products for the mass market. And it probably never will be. We are not interested."

My peace of mind: the Liebaert management team of Daniel, Kevin, Philippe, Luc and Greet.

LOOKING TO THE FUTURE

After COVID-19 clears, things might be better. Hopefully! There will be scarcity, and people will want to buy high-quality, long-lasting goods from nearby, for all kinds of reasons – sustainability issues, transport issues and concern about carbon emissions. The question is, though, are consumers ready to pay 50–100% more for their textiles? Or will the whole ethical sustainability bandwagon be completely abandoned when everything gets too expensive?

I am confident that our turnover will climb back up to €25 million by the end of 2023. My confidence comes from our diversification efforts – primarily, our branded projects: RectoVerso and RV-Elite.

RectoVerso (www.rectoversosports.com) has a unique design touch and high-quality fabrics that make it stand out in the athleisure fashion world. A lot of fashion and sports gurus are already fans of our brand. It's the only athleisure brand completely made in Belgium.

RV-Elite (www.rvecompression.com) is a high-tech compression garment developed in conjunction with the Sport Science Laboratory – Jacques Rogge at Ghent University after more than five years of research with top athletes. The garment is made out of a unique Weftlock fabric and we have developed a patented compression algorithm that protects muscles during exertion and helps them recover faster. A lot of Belgian Olympic athletes are our ambassadors already. We are seeing quite a revolution in the world of sports garments!

So, thanks to our foray into the world of garment-making, through our own locally made athleisure brand, we have a couple of aces in our hand in the burgeoning landscape of ethical consumerism. More will perhaps materialize in the future.

A second consideration for the future is that many of our weaker competitors are disappearing and at the same time new customers in technical textiles are emerging. The logistics chaos created by COVID-19, with container prices increasing tenfold and raw materials ballooning, has brought new opportunities for financially strong local producers like ourselves. The importance of being a local and reliable supplier is becoming paramount for our existing customers. All being well, our EBITDA should reach 25% again.

The view of Kevin, our COO, is: "I see us being a very healthy company in the future, even after all these very difficult years. We've survived several crises really well and I think in the next couple of years we're going to get more chances and opportunities than ever. The growing momentum of RectoVerso is some indication of where we may be going. In five to ten years, we'll have a healthy company still making money, but we will perhaps work in different markets, or at least produce greater turnover in new markets."

It's clear now, I hope, that turnover is no longer the tell-tale sign of success – there are so many other measurements to accommodate. You must know all your numbers if you have any intention of surviving. Look at their evolution – see how they change over time. Through this comparison, you can ascertain whether you're heading in the right direction or not.

I'm pleased to say that over my 30-year career as CEO, Liebaert Textiles has constantly increased its profitability despite going from growth to steep decline. Since the 1980s and over two generations, we have built a company that is not only extremely creative but also extremely profitable.

For all the magician's tricks and Hail Marys we've pulled out to do this, read Part Two. For now, let's have a quick look at how family businesses differ from others before visiting a few of my chosen CEOs' helpful anecdotes.

FAMILY BUSINESSES VS OTHERS

There are both many similarities and many differences between businesses that are run by families and those that aren't. It's very tricky to say which is better. In general, family businesses look at things with a much longer perspective; this means they make more conservative decisions and are therefore better weaponized to survive decline.

The sad truth tells us, though, that the complicated interwoven relationships between family stakeholders often reap irreparable damage. This puts a huge burden on the poor soul who needs to navigate the business through the emotionally charged minefield.

Many listed companies, in contrast, have a short-term strategy to profit and grow. Their management usually fixates on figures and bonuses, often demonstrating minimal emotional connection to

the company and its greater story and ethos –
either that or they poorly ape fondness and affec-
tion for these elements. Don't have these 'hired
guns' in your crew if you want to defeat decline
and master the minus. To ride back to profit, you
need emotionally committed, loyal utility players,
whether they're family or not.

While family businesses are more resilient in times
of crisis – it's a proven fact – a lot of the treacherous
pitfalls that besiege them remain present regard-
less. However, provided the company has a strong
family member who has an undisputed remit to
lead everyone through troubled waters, there's a
good chance of survival. Opting for the contrary,
and choosing an outsider to run things might
work, but it's certainly a more precarious strategy.

Be mindful and recognize that if unity of command is splintered and lost, disaster lurks around
the next corner, smirking. If responsibilities must
be doled out and shared – purely to please family
members – you're in real trouble. Keep command
solid. Leave it in the possession of *one* person.

However, even if this leader has considerable
respect around the business, if they are rusty and
worn out, impervious to a changing world, this
will be another huge threat to survival. When
the CEO becomes unsuitable, the big question is
who objectively assesses the leadership? The other
question, of course, is will the leader even listen?

The most expedient approach involves either a
trusted outsider whispering gently in the CEO's ear,

encouraging change, or the younger generations taking it upon themselves to respectfully challenge management. The latter is what happened in my experience. I'm very grateful to my children for their sense and strength in challenging me from time to time.

You need to have a thorough understanding of your own knowledge. But you must also know your knowledge's limits. What *don't* you know? An awareness of what's missing from your thinking is an invaluable, life-saving weapon in your arsenal. Be ready. Be prepared. Expect to step aside *before* your company, your community and your family ask for it. Don't get blindsided because of your own ego.

So, with all that in mind, *if* all tasks are clearly delineated, all noses are pointing in the same direction *and* there's no – or minimal – frustration or jealousy, a family business will fare better in decline than the alternative. However, that's a heavy set of demands and, as I'm sure you'll imagine, a very rare situation. Sadly, even in the best cases, family businesses typically last a generation or two.

A final point concerns romantic intimacy – in other words, couples. Having a couple running a business together is an absolute NO GO in most organizations as it is. But in a declining company, avoid having a couple in charge at all costs. It is practically impossible to remain objective and it can lead to bias in your relationships with other team members. This arrangement can destroy relationships within a company, not to mention

– more pertinently – in a family. Personal issues will cloud your judgment and blind you. You want to have the clearest view you can when traversing a storm.

In many ways, my extraordinary wife would have been a much better boss than me. She would have been an invaluable asset to our company, but she chose to stay out and build a unique and happy family instead. In hindsight, this was without a doubt the best choice for everybody involved!

SUCCESSION

If you're operating a family business, ensure that your succession rules and policies are extremely stringent and well defined. Two of the most important things to consider are:
1. Getting consensus in the family
2. Getting management to accept the consensus

The criteria in our company, where there were two branches of the family running the company in tandem for a couple of generations, was that only one member of each immediate family should be co-CEO. Both individuals had to have a university degree, while evidencing that they had picked up other skills at the same time as studying. It was incumbent on them to train in some capacity at the company during their studies, too – which, in some part, fulfilled the previous criterion of gaining new skills. Outside experience was the final feature of a presumptive Liebaert CEO – five years was great, if possible, and certainly more than two.

Today, all of the above expectations remain; however, there's now a key difference that should do a great deal to shape our future as a company – there is only one CEO. No more bicephalism. At times the strain and conflict were monstrous, but now, thankfully, after 100 years, they have been resolved. From now on, Liebaert will have one member at the head.

I believe a final fundamental rule is that the CEO should step down long before they become a burden and to keep vitality and sustainable action in the company.

There are still some unsolvable issues. Of course, those family members who work in the company and those who don't will experience discrepancies in remuneration, which generates an endless spiral of frustrations. Who is more valuable than whom to the company also remains a completely intractable equation that none of us can ever solve. Within family, 'value' is, naturally, a very different beast from how it is perceived in non-family businesses.

If you're in a family business hampered by an internal conflict or stalemate, there's one big question you must ask yourself. Are you ready to sacrifice family ties to secure the company's future? It's an agonizing debate and there is no right answer.

Essentially, it comes down to this: would you rather saddle your children with a declining company at the risk of destroying family harmony forever, or safely and slowly manoeuvre toward an exit strategy? It is always sad to end a legacy, but it's better than extending a bitter one that might alienate you from your spouse, children and possibly even grandchildren.

I have worked with a lot of family businesses, both suppliers and customers. There are also a lot of family businesses in my private circles. And I have *never* encountered one free from some sort of generations-old dispute or quarrel. While a few have continued very successfully, they have all lost a lot of energy and time in unnecessary friction.

GO OR NO GO: STORIES OF EXTRAORDINARY CEOS

As I said in my introduction, I want to dedicate a section to the extraordinary CEOs who have contributed to my development – through their flaws and failures just as much as (if not more than) their wins and victories. Here are a few of their stories. Some are GOs; some are NO GOs. Either way, they are all lessons.

FAMILY BURNOUT

FAMILY BUSINESSES: MORE NO GO THAN GO

Mr X had the charm and creativity necessary to develop one of the most successful brands in his industry. Both director and minority shareholder, he put exceptional effort into the company

– his family's company – excelling at sales and product development. Unfortunately, continuous family issues within the company caused Mr X to experience burnout and he left at around the age of 50. His departure was a major loss and a great shame for his company and our industry.

CLOSING SLOWLY

Mr Y was a very charming, honest man. He was a delight to do business with. When his garment business began to decline, he wisely decided to close his company over a period of five years. This staggered shutdown gave his employees, suppliers and customers ample time to organize themselves. He left as a gentleman, ready to enjoy his old age.

CLOSING A COMPANY WHEN YOU STILL CAN: GO

BOWING OUT GRACEFULLY

One of our biggest customers supplied M&S from its ten UK factories. The boss was quite eccentric; he loved classic cars and, as a pilot himself, shared my enthusiasm for flying. Unsurprisingly, we became good friends. He sold his company two years before M&S chose to move production to East Asia. Within five years, all his factories were closed. In hindsight, he saw the exit sign right on time.

LEAVING THE WATER BEFORE THE STORM: GO

NICE IS NOT ENOUGH

BEING
TOO NICE:
NO GO

Mr Z was an old-school French gentleman who ran the best fabric-printing operation in our trade. He was very cultivated; he cared about his workers and respected his customers, even to the detriment of his own company. For me, he was the model example of a good human being – I envied his class and kindness. But those were the very qualities that brought him down. He went bankrupt. Given that there were few good printing alternatives in his wake, we started our own. It was another great shame.

COUPLES IN COMPANIES

WORKING
WITH
COUPLES:
NO GO

A good friend and I are partners in a tourism business. My friend is a very smart operator, a talented salesperson and someone who understands numbers. He is a pleasure to work with but unfortunately his life partner is also involved in the business, which has sparked constant friction and left a sour aftertaste.

ANOTHER NICE GUY

LEAVING
A FAMILY
BUSINESS
DUE TO
CONFLICT:
GO

BEING
TOO NICE:
NO GO

Because of the inevitable constant family quarrels, Mr A left a big family textile business to create his own little print shop. He was a very nice, sympathetic and kind man who developed his business quite well in the good years. Like Mr Z, he was a very good boss as well as technically strong. But, fatally, he was far too nice to personnel, customers and suppliers. When the bad years came along, he went bankrupt.

KNOW WHEN TO GO

Mr B sold his successful aviation company to a big financial group. He stayed in the company for a while after selling, which didn't go very well. He was quite eccentric, a man who enjoyed life to the fullest and had immense industry knowledge. He was also a very good and honest businessman who knew his numbers. His one flaw was his bad judgment about people – consequently, he was surrounded by weak and egotistical people to whom he couldn't delegate, meaning he had to do everything himself. The new owners took poor care of his company, causing him great frustration from the sidelines, as he saw what he had built suffering without being able to do anything about it.

BAD PEOPLE JUDGMENT: NO GO

STAYING TOO LONG: NO GO

A MISMATCHED MERGER

Mr C had both a law degree and a notary degree but didn't pursue a legal career. Instead, he was the director of a European bank branch in our city for about ten years, until he decided to buy a transport company with his brother. They specialized in transporting exceptional and oversized loads, often private yachts, even though they knew nothing about this sector. Within a few years, though, Mr C was an expert.

MERGING WITH THE WRONG PARTNER: NO GO

He was also a fervent sailor and a very sociable man, being a member of many social and philosophical clubs. Unfortunately, he merged his business with a fellow transporter who proved to be a completely dysfunctional, anti-social person.

After three years of uninterrupted friction, the company went bankrupt. What remained of the company was sold to a French group with big visions about the future of transport in Western Europe – definitely another declining sector if you ask me! The group went bankrupt after a few years – a perfect example of hubris.

TRAGEDY AT THE HEART OF TEXTILES

MISTAKING SIZE FOR SUCCESS: NO GO

FAMILY BUSINESSES: MORE NO GO THAN GO

Mr D married F, the daughter of one of the biggest French textile groups' bosses. He himself eventually became CEO of the group, much to his brother-in-law's umbrage and disapproval. Her brother's behaviour was very hurtful for F, who was a brilliant doctor and professor, a loving wife and a doting mother. Her father fired Mr D and installed his son as CEO. This led to huge family issues, which of course involved lawyers. In the end, F couldn't cope any more and tragically took her own life.

Looking for revenge and a salve for his ego, Mr D decided to build a big textile group through aggressive acquisition. He wanted to prove that he could succeed in life without his in-laws. He became our biggest competitor and we became friends. Revenge clouds good decision-making, though, and his group went bankrupt after 20 years.

His biggest mistake was obsessing over 'big' instead of focusing on being profitable. Being profitable is far more important than size, but this was a very common mistake in the pre-COVID-19 business world. Before, size was the main marker of success.

The first thing Stalin asked world leaders he met was, "How many divisions?" Is this the world we want to live in, where size overshadows everything else?

DREAM ON

Mr E and Mr G were both egotistical dreamers in two different sectors. They were masters of bullshit, always building chimeras and convincing credulous investors to invest more and more money. Their only interest in finance lay in window-dressing their balance sheets and putting more money in their own pockets to attract more credulous investors (I was one of them). Always beware of bullshit and dreamers, especially in a declining company – you just can't afford the risk.

FALLING FOR BULLSHIT: NO GO

I sincerely hope that a necessary shift in people's mentalities happens. This shift would enable families and decent people to work together for a common goal while sharing kindness and love. To my knowledge, up to now at least, those virtues have been absent from declining businesses, leading to failures and devastation. If we can make this shift, the future could look very different. There would be far more GOs than NO GOs.

CONCLUSION

Now you know what happened to us – doctors and lawyers, brewers and bankers – from Alfred's adventures in Africa to a mill set up by boys, two world wars, bombs and rebuilds, family feuds and early deaths, steep decline caused by an Asian chimera, 20 years of downsizing for survival, COVID-19, mayoral requests for masks and hopefully recovery in the shape of finished garments.

I'm confident you can extract the many lessons present in our more than a century of stories. You can combine them with the varied experiences of my extraordinary CEO chorus to get a complete picture of how to defeat not just decline, but other threats to your business too. Whether yours is a family business or not, old or new, big or small, provided it's one in decline, the stories you've heard so far can help you to frame the instructions and advice in the next part of this book.

Part 2

MANAGING
DECLINE

There were many reasons for our decline – some of them political (crisis), some of them psychological (family frictions) and others economic. However, none of them were as decisive as the shift of the manufacturing industry to Asia, and China in particular.

The everlasting quest for lower costs and cheap labour made the textile industry the first victim in this new economic order. Our customer base was melting like snow under the sun and we were unable to reinvent ourselves or adapt quickly enough to prevent decline.

As you have seen in the previous sections, our decline was partly the consequence of deliberate decisions we took. The most significant one was not to relocate our production facilities to Asia. So, you could say that we were partly responsible for our own decline, and you would be right. We decided to play chess without a queen. However, as this part of the book will show, if you are a good player, you can survive long enough to drive your opponent into a stalemate.

" Revenue is Vanity, Profit is Sanity and Cash is King. "

– Alan Miltz

A FEW INITIAL PREMISES

Before we talk in detail about the intricacies of surviving in decline, there are a few general premises that should be accepted by anyone in this position if they are going to cope at all. These pieces of advice will equip you with all the insights necessary to manage your company with a clear vision in tough times:

- **Nobody has a fucking clue what's coming next.**
  Seriously. This has never been clearer than in COVID-19 times.
- **Consider all probable eventualities.**
  You will be better prepared and sleep better at night. Doing the hard work upfront makes the future easier. Quantity breeds quality, as you'll see in the section below about creativity.
- **Know what you're prepared to lose.**
  When you make decisions, always think: if this fails, what am I prepared to lose? *Don't* think: how much will I profit if this succeeds?
- **Think about the worst-case scenario first.**
  This philosophy is *the* basic principle in controlling a declining company.

- **Being worried is healthy; being stressed is unhealthy.**
  There's a difference: it's about being ahead of the curve or behind the curve.
- **Forget about the visionary billionaires.**
  This book does not take them into account. For every lucky exception, there are 100,000 hard-working 'normal' people who use everyday management skills.
- **Be entrepreneurial, know your product and have the guts to take strategic action.**
  If you have a certain degree of all these qualities, then you're going to fare as well as you can. They are the prerequisites for you to succeed.
- **Be intuitive, but don't be impulsive.**
  Don't make life-changing decisions too hastily. Look for what can be cancelled or revised if necessary, especially in view of the very uncertain conditions that lie ahead of us in the COVID-19 world. A lot of so-called economic, financial and social 'rules' and 'theories' could soon change drastically, so the department you close or the product you drop might be what saves your life in the new economy.
- **But don't forget – doing nothing is far worse than making bad decisions.**
  We can learn and gain experience from our bad decisions. This can help an upcoming project succeed, but only because the first one failed.

A FEW INITIAL QUESTIONS

"*Success is walking from failure to failure with no loss of enthusiasm.*"

– anonymous,
commonly attributed to Winston Churchill

If you're running a declining company, or you're considering taking on the serious commitment of doing so, ask yourself these questions:

- Does it or will it make me happy?
- Do I want to proceed?
- Do I have a *very* good reason to proceed?
- What is that reason?
- How old am I both physically and mentally?

- It is going to be a marathon. Am I in the perfect physical and psychological health to go through this?
- Do I have the required abilities to lead my team through challenging times?
- Do I have the resilience and patience to master decline?
- Do I have a capable, committed, faithful and agile team that will follow me through hell and put their careers aside for the long-term goal?
- Will my team jump ship when the shit hits the fan?
- If I have a younger team, is this more of a risk?
- Am I ready to involve my team in all decisions and be totally transparent even if this means bringing bad news?
- Do I have the personnel to resize or restructure?
- Do I have enough cash to go through this period or is my company highly indebted? (Negotiating some long-term debt can be an option, although it is certainly not my favourite one.)
- Does my product have a future in the market?
- What's my work–life balance? Do I have the necessary downtime to think about all possible scenarios?
- Am I ready to lead by example and be on the deck of my ship every working day when in stormy waters?
- Do I love my company, my product, my team?

"

Working hard for something we don't care about is called stress; working hard for something we love is called passion.

"

– Simon Sinek

If you answered no to any of the above questions, seriously consider doing one of the following:
1. Selling your company (another long and painful process)
2. Closing your company (if you have enough cash, simply stopping is an elegant solution)

In the worst case, you can let your company go bankrupt, but this is never a socially acceptable choice and we won't be discussing that here.

Some big groups are experts at squeezing everything out of their employees, their suppliers and their government, but their only objective is to take the maximum amount of cash out of the company. This is neither an ethical nor a sustainable solution. If you're in that position, this book is not for you.

Your answers to these questions may waver and change – but stay strong if you ever said no to any of these questions and decided to proceed against the odds. If you fight hard enough, you will find the light at the end of the tunnel.

Now, let's have a look at what you should concentrate on to successfully manage a company in decline.

PILOT'S EMERGENCY CHECKLIST: FLYING FOR SURVIVAL

See your company like a vehicle manoeuvring through the elements. Whether it's a plane, a ship or a rickshaw, you must keep it moving or it will crash. You are the captain; you are the pilot; you're driving the vehicle. If you don't want to nosedive, hit the bottom or tumble off the road, you have to keep cool and maintain command. Too many captains cause a crash.

I had a very good flying instructor, one of the best. He was a chief pilot on jumbo jets for years and now he works for the Belgian aviation authority and does all of the country's air accident investigations. He always told me, "Alain, if anything ever goes wrong and the whole cockpit lights up like a Christmas tree, first take a deep breath and get out a cigarette," (in those days, pilots could smoke). He continued: "Next you think, and *then* you act. If you start pushing buttons without thinking, then you'll surely die."

The main thing is to be in control. You must remain calm and disciplined, then consider what might be happening. Be intuitive, not impulsive. When you are in a very high-risk environment, there's more time than you think, and panicked actions will only precipitate your trip south. Panic never works.

Nor is such an occasion best handled by a 'community council' approach. In the case of flying, the pilot – with the copilot's support – must be trusted to get everyone out of trouble on their own. My family and I once had a dramatic journey that helps to illustrate the need to keep cool and maintain command.

It was the first time I flew my family over Iceland and Greenland. We were in a twin prop, which my son Andre said was like a 'flying houseboat.' It was night-time and we'd been flying for hours at −68°C with very little ground time, so the fuel tanks hadn't had much chance to warm up.

Fuel ices up at about −47°C and the fuel heaters in twin props don't work very well. As our fuel began approaching −44°C, it started to become a heavy sludge and it wouldn't go through the fuel pump.

The whole plane was flying like a brick when one engine began sputtering. We weren't too alarmed – we knew we could get to Greenland with one engine if needed. But, as we were beginning to lose the first one, the second started sputtering too. My copilot and I instantly went as white as sheets of paper. The whole family was in the back!

Rather than losing composure and screaming, hammering away at the control panels like mad-men and alerting the whole family in the process, we stopped what we were doing and collected our thoughts. The likelihood of losing two engines at the same time is almost zero, unless there's fuel icing. So, we dropped a few thousand feet to where it was warmer, and we recuperated both engines. We never really lost either, but they were on their way out. It was a simple solution, once we took a minute to think.

My copilot, who is now in his late fifties and has 15,000 hours as a pilot over 30 years, told me recently that our icing incident was the most frightening experience he's ever had in an air-plane. It was mine, too. Luckily, my family didn't break a sweat. They had very little idea of what was going on, because in that moment, we were the pilots and they were the passengers. If we kept calm, they'd be calm. If we maintained command, they wouldn't confuse things or distract us as we worked out what to do.

Andre was five when the flying houseboat almost lost its momentum. But for him, this memory isn't such a scary one. He wasn't the only one unphased, it seems. Here's what he had to say about the incident recently:

> I remember my grandmother woke up from a sleep, and my mum told her what was happening, to which she said, "Ah, well we still have the other engine luckily." That's the spirit, right? That was one of our very close calls.
>
> But my dad is one of the best pilots I've ever seen. Touch wood. I'm a bit more conscious now of how crazy it is, but when I was younger, Dad flying the plane seemed normal. We all just have so much faith in him.
>
> It's like with the company, too – if there's a problem, "Dad will fix it." This puts a lot of pressure on him, but I hope it also gives him great confidence.

Many of these lessons can be applied to business. Of course, while running a company can be like flying a plane, there are far fewer chances of fatal consequences. However, as you've seen already, if you don't do it right, there can be tragedies.

If you don't want to nosedive, there are a few areas you should consider:

1. **People.**

   Who do you have around you? This is crucial. You *must* delegate – have people around you that you have confidence in.

2. **Product.**

   What are you selling? Who to? How do you do it? Know every part of the process.

3. **Structure.**

   How is your organization structured from the people and management points of view? Can it be improved? If so, restructure from the top down.

4. **Money.**

   How much do you have? How is it flowing? Banks might not always be there when you need them, so you have to have your own financial infrastructure.

5. **Evaluation.**

   What is it all worth? You need to know the numbers. All in all, when you do the maths, what is the value of all your assets? How do you measure them?

6. **Outside forces.**

   What could cause you trouble from the outside? Keep a close eye on those forces and navigate around them safely.

OK, let's go!

1. PEOPLE

Nobody will dispute that human capital and inter-action are the keys to successful businesses. This is especially true if you want to successfully master decline. But how should you behave as the boss? You must consider what's expected of you as well as what you expect of your employees, suppliers and customers.

INTERNALLY

You have no greater asset than the people inside your company. Know what they need to be happy, healthy and successful in their roles. Know what's expected of you as the boss and how to help your employees excel. Have a system or framework in mind that guarantees effective performance – for me, this comes from teaching, training, delegating and motivating, as you'll see shortly.

As people are the most valuable assets in any organization, we are constantly looking to sur-round ourselves with the best and the most intel-ligent people so as to build the strongest possible team. This usually takes a lifetime!

But what kind of 'intelligence' are we looking for? The desired kind of intelligence has the following characteristics:

- Humility – this is *the* essential trait of intelligence; when you have nothing to say, shut up!
- Knowledge of your abilities
- Knowledge of your flaws and shortcomings
- The ability to surround yourself with complementary colleagues
- The ability to analyse complex problems and situations, and then synthesize them
- The ability to explain complex problems simply to laypeople
- The ability to sense other people's emotional intelligence
- Social intelligence, which involves comfortably navigating a blend of circumstances, cultures and religions

If you can create a team that naturally has these virtues, you can be certain to weather any storm that comes your way!

BEING THE BOSS

> **"Try not to become a man of success but rather try to become a man of value."**
>
> **Albert Einstein**

Is the 'ultimate leader' and 'all-powerful parent' archetype of a boss something people want and need in an organization? Is such a role necessary for a company to prosper?

Most organizations, and most people really, like to hang their hat on a strong hook – one that gives them confidence. It gives them energy and comfort, and a sense of safety. They sleep better at night knowing someone is looking out for them and guaranteeing their future.

Of course, a lot of CEOs take this too far and become angry tyrants, which defeats the purpose. Yet the line between the two is very thin. The "I'm the captain now" syndrome, as in the film *Captain Phillips* (2013), takes over very easily.

What are the traits of the 'ultimate leader' type of boss?

- **Genuinely interested in many things.**
  Their knowledge must go far beyond the business aspects of life. The broader their interests, the more they will be able to tap into their knowledge database when the shit hits the fan.
- **Genuinely interested in their people, what they do and who they are.**
  This boss tries to understand their people. They always have time for their most valuable resources: their spouse or partner, kids, friends, management and workers.
- **The ultimate time manager.**
  They must have plenty of time for their team and their own personal development, and they

must be the 'watchtower' of the company. This means they should constantly have an overview of everything and everybody. When my father died, the only way I could get a grasp of my organization was to meet with my various teams (quality control, planning, and research and development) once a week and with my sales team and my COO once every day. All issues were noticed immediately and dealt with. My team knew exactly what I expected from them.

- **The ability to do a 'role swap' and show genuine empathy for the members of their team.**
  Ideally, the leader should be able to do all the work of their direct subordinates. This makes them less dependent on the subordinates while also showing respect and understanding of their problems. My many traineeships in the company during my school holidays were invaluable in enabling me to understand all aspects of the organization.

- **No mood swings and total impartiality.**
  When I entered the company with two bosses (my father and his cousin), each one had their favourites which, of course, led to frictions, jealousies and political games within management. This is an absolute NO GO!

- **Courageous.**
  This is a trait of my son Mathieu: you don't walk away from trouble and you back your team in *any* circumstances. Too many bosses are cowards, hiding behind their title and letting their minions do the dirty work.

Here's some insight about me from my daughter, Camille, who is today a brand manager in the company:

He is transparent and keeps everyone informed, whether it is good or bad news. He encourages people to take initiative and takes full responsibility when making difficult decisions. And he will never look back thinking we should've done differently.

His most important asset? Composure. He is always prepared and remains calm, even when shit hits the fan. This became all the more apparent to me in COVID-19 times.

Last but not least, he is passionate. He is as generous in his praise as he is strict in his feedback. But then again, with my father, you always know where you stand. Therefore, it's his honesty that sets him apart; not only toward his employees, but also toward customers and suppliers. I would call this his trademark in business.

GENERAL PHILOSOPHY
The way I manage the people inside my business operates through a simple four-part process:
- **Teach:** tell them what you want them to do
- **Train:** show them how to do it
- **Delegate:** let them get on with it
- **Motivate:** encourage them so they do well

Good teamwork comes with highly trained staff who know what they're doing. Learning comes from talking, showing and doing. Have trust and understanding with the people in your company. Tell them what's going on, what decisions you've made and why you made them. Tell them their part in the play. Don't breed a culture of fear and secrecy – it never ends well, *believe me*.

I have learned one golden rule about people as a management consultant and then the CEO of a company in long-term decline: *if you treat people like assholes, they will act like assholes*. In 99% of cases, the reason for failure is that management didn't train their people well enough or showed blatant disrespect when interacting with them.

Therefore, before you reorganize your company, thoroughly assess your management team. You should closely assess and measure not only their skills but also, and even more importantly, their attitudes and values – failure to do this is often where disaster lies in businesses.

When you reorganize, you should do it from top to bottom – not, as most companies do, the other way around. This route is, of course, far more expensive, but it repays itself a hundredfold in the long run.

My most efficient results have come from discarding management completely and starting from scratch again with (often) unskilled but very committed workers. It is much easier to motivate somebody at a lower level than highly paid, rusty managers with big egos and fancy degrees.

Your company's gold lies in the lower-level labour force. Use them wisely, motivate them and incentivize them, and you'll see much better results, much faster than if you gave that attention to management instead.

Another big debate is whether specialists or generalists are better at doing the job of CEO. In my experience, a person can become a decent generalist in three to six months' time, except in very technical jobs such as IT, biomedicine or aerospace. I will always prefer a flexible generalist that has a general knowledge of finance (an absolute must if you want to manage decline), IT, marketing and production processes over a rusty super-specialist in any of these fields.

Some advice:
- Treat your staff as equals while remaining their leader
- Be totally transparent and tell them as much as they need to know
- Teach them about cost prices and efficiency
- Give them *all* the numbers – that includes sales, profits and quality
- Explain to them *what* you're going to do, *why* you're going to do it and, very importantly, what *their* crucial role is in achieving the objective
- Remember that non-financial incentives relating to mental and physical wellbeing, as well as access to a healthy work–life balance, are becoming even more important than financial ones in our changing society (so, consider a dinner, an activity, more free time, etc.)

However, in the end, somebody needs to make the decisions, and democracy does not work in a company. You'll have to be assertive and charismatic. It is the only way to have your team behind you.

"Tell me and I forget. Teach me and I remember. Involve me and I learn."

anonymous,
commonly attributed to Confucius

HIRING VERSUS INTERNAL PROMOTION

Whether you bring in new blood or refresh what you already have is an important decision. Really consider the implications. For my company, promotion has many more merits, which I'll soon explain. There is no perfect formula – a lot falls to fate and you need a touch of trial and error to establish what suits you best.

We have heated discussions among the management of my company before hiring new people. In a declining company in a declining sector, hiring people, especially managers, is a big challenge. We basically only have two types of candidate to fill the gaps in our business:

- Type one is young and usually doesn't stay very long. They work hard for less money than they could get elsewhere in the market, while still having a lot to learn and a desire to go and do it.
- Type two is experienced and expensive. This type is often rusty and doesn't adapt easily to an established company philosophy.

Our industry's hiring problem is compounded by a further detail, mentioned in part one. Owing to the mass production migration East, there has been little need or desire for training in textiles in Europe in the 21st century, not to mention many other skills and professions. There are no textile schools now, meaning we often have to hire managers who have absolutely no experience or understanding of our product.

We then lose at least two years training them, taking valuable time from our other, already overworked staff. But even after our thorough screening and training, only 10% of them stay in the company for more than five years.

They have almost no added value in the first two years while costing about €150,000. This money is then lost if (and, sadly, more usually when) they leave the company. We have hired ten people over the past five years, of whom only one has stayed. This means we have lost €1.35 million training the nine who left.

In contrast, there are a lot of advantages when we try to have one of our workers climb the ladder:

- They know the product, the people and the organization and we know their character and abilities
- We only really have to invest time, not money
- If it's a failed experiment and they're more suitable for their former job, they can simply move back to that position

In this second scenario, we have had a success rate of 50%.

Do the maths!

WOMEN

Business has room for far more women and far more diversity. While things are changing, the pace is tardy and a lot of what we're seeing in the way of these things from big enterprises is largely symbolic. Getting the best women into business is instrumental in changing the typically hostile and competitive climate, where dog eats dog and we're at war.

I have been let down and disappointed many times in my career. Most times, it was by a man. For this reason, I've always surrounded myself with women, both personally and professionally.

Call it an old-fashioned opinion, but I think by nature, women are on average more empathetic. This is something I've witnessed in abundance across my career. As such, women should be appreciated and valued for the fact that they are women

– for their *differences* from men. Stereotypically feminine qualities (which, of course, may be found in any person) in society complement and control stereotypically masculine qualities.

Here are some general insights I've had about the many women whom I've encountered deftly manoeuvring through the very cold and cruel landscapes of business (which I've suffered and struggled through myself too). By no means do I wish for this list to be seen as a set of definitive facts; these are just my thoughts and observations. But I think there is an enormous amount we can learn from analysing these characteristics:

1. Women tend to be humble in their intelligence
2. Women tend not to be weakened by being empathetic
3. Women tend to have greater endurance than men but less resistance to stress
4. Women tend to look for compromises rather than conflicts
5. Women can put their egos aside
6. Women tend to be loyal and will stick with you, even when times get tough
7. Women tend to be far less incentivized by money

These are among many reasons why I think we need far more women in business in general, but especially in a company that faces great adversity and devastating business conditions. In situations like those, there is no place for ego.

To some extent, the ego – which, as suggested above, tends to be a masculine thing – can be very good if you want growth in business. As a boss, you need to be a little megalomaniacal. Most bosses are. It's proven. I am convinced that you need to be a bit egotistical to be a successful leader.

So, I'm not saying that all 'male' traits are negative and all 'female' traits are positive.

But it is rather clear that if the world were run by a greater share of women, it would probably be a better place and we would have most likely avoided many of the conflicts masterminded by men.

All I am saying is that stereotypically feminine qualities should be used more, but this should not create an anti-masculine atmosphere. Generating one risks destroying those very qualities that make women so unique and so powerful in their own right. We just need to even the balance.

But this won't happen with quotas. I know a lot of women who are on a board of directors and think the policy of having all boards half male and half female is ridiculous and counter-intuitive. Some of them have been as bold as to say that it's the biggest bullshit in the world. You should have the best board. It's not about being a man or being a woman. You should have the best *people* on your board.

Choose those people with the best abilities, but also those with whom you have the strongest human connection – those who'll happily do things for you and whom you'd happily do things for in return. A business needs this symbiosis – one that's almost oblivious to hierarchy, status and division.

Everyone is equally important, even if there is only one boss.

"COFFEE, BOSS?"

Is being nice to each other the new NO GO? It sure seems so. Here's an example.

I have a lot of burden as a boss – especially lately, what with buying my cousin out of the business (as described in Part One). My staff are loyal and aware of this, and do whatever they can to make my life just that little bit easier. So one morning, my old secretary, Greet, who is now my CSO, brought me a coffee. No big deal, right?

Apparently, it's a big deal! My son and daughter could not believe their eyes – they thought this was something from a completely different day and age. Not only was it 'sexist' – or something vaguely in that territory – but it was also generally demeaning and a vestige of an obsolete business model where the boss is the patriarch and his employees must fear and serve him ...

But no, this was absolutely not what was going on when Greet brought me that cup of coffee.

No matter who does it, I appreciate it when someone brings me a coffee.

Nonetheless, I told my staff that they didn't need to do it any more. But they said, "We like doing it. And we know you like it." They think it's nice, too! It's mutual. They don't feel diminished because they've brought me a coffee. It makes for human connection.

And that's what we risk losing when we throw out little gestures such as this: that human connection.

DIVERSITY

We must recognize other countries' talents. As there are no European textile schools left and many Europeans don't want to work in a declining sector, our company has hired a lot of workers from different countries. Their skills, enthusiasm and respect have always been a huge motivating factor for me.

Many of my very talented employees are from Turkey (25%) and about 10% are from somewhere else beyond Europe, such as Afghanistan, Albania or Tunisia.

Having a diverse workforce helps to display a fundamental truth: that we can work together. We're better when we simply look for nice people who are ready to work. Nothing else matters. Not religion, race, gender or sexuality. I wasn't brought up that way. Whatever, and whoever, works best.

Being brought up and exposed to a wide range of different people makes for an easier time, a more enjoyable time. There's less hate and anger. There's more excitement and enthusiasm – more people to have a close relationship with.

Chancellor Angela Merkel of Germany is a great example of a leader who can take us to a more inclusive future – partly because she's a woman, and partly because of her life and her experiences. I have so much respect for her. She was brought up in

East Germany, which was hardly a paradise. Because of that, perhaps, she doesn't seem to need a lot personally. She's not money hungry. She's not power hungry. She's very genuine when she talks.

'Mutti' (as she is commonly known in Germany and beyond) is a very pragmatic woman; I like that. What she did with welcoming Syrians into Europe was very brave. She genuinely believed that we couldn't leave people dying on our doorstep or instead give billions to Turkey to keep them there rather than actually helping them out.

This is a sign of the empathetic world my management team and I want to live in. We should be kind to everybody, not just our own people. This will help from an economic point of view too. It has helped my industry, because I'm short of people who sew. I can't find them. In Syria, there are many, many people who sew. They are all very welcome!

MANAGING RISK AND EGOS

There are two primary things you'll have to manage in a company fighting for survival: risk and egos. The two aren't dissimilar and they can have equally grave impacts on a company's core if they are not readily assessed.

Know the hazards and calculate your worst-case scenarios. Look for options and possibilities. Out of all crises arise huge opportunities. Take the time to open your eyes and see them. Remember to take care of yourself – meditation, relaxation, travel and a change of scenery are all invaluable and essential for you, your family and your company.

Know how to handle blackmail situations from management, and always look to replace ability with flexibility. Organize a multi-tooled and multi-informed management structure. Keep as many people as possible in the loop. It might seem inefficient at first, but you honestly do sleep better at night when you're not dependent on a few individually skilled managers.

Most managers have big egos and a lot of neuroses. But these qualities can be necessary, often because they are what drive people. Like the antigens in our bodies, which are there to fight infections, these parts of someone's personality ensure their survival. But, if they take over, the person will die from within.

Handling the egos in your organization is key to managing risk. If they're not kept under control, they can do irrevocable damage. As the boss, you're not above the law, either – everyone keeps each other's egos balanced.

THE IMPORTANCE OF REST

Professional pilots have to take courses on physiology and study the importance of rest. Doing so protects our performance when we are discharging our duties as crew members. We have to abide by our duty and rest times, and there are dire consequences if we don't respect them.

A normal shift, from arriving at the airport to leaving it, is 13 hours. Many accidents in aviation have been the consequence of tired crews. In life and in business more generally, too, many failures find their origin in tired, overstressed people. The problem isn't always the quantity of sleep, but the quality.

The quality of our sleep is often disregarded, despite it being an even more important factor than the duration of our sleep. Overlooking sleep quality can have chronic implications for all areas of our work and home life. Abuse it at your own risk. And know your own limits, as well as the limits to which we're all subject.

It's been proven that if we're actively concentrating and efficiently busy for more than eight hours, our performance begins to deteriorate rapidly. Certain business philosophies in both the East and the West are practised by people who pride themselves on working 16 hours a day. These attitudes are not only inefficient; they are wasting people's lives and preventing them from enjoying quality family time.

A lot of lost time comes from overly long meetings where people pontificate endlessly. I have spent many hours in these meaningless meetings, where people only wish to prove how busy they are. This 'myth of busy' must go. What many of us call 'busy' is really just being disorganized and inefficient with time. In most cases, efficient decisions could have been made in a fraction of the time. What a waste!

We work too many hours and sleep too few. To do the first of these well, we desperately need the second. Our mind and body need rest to be able to cope with stress, to act swiftly without hesitation and to stay alert for a long time.

A sleep cycle lasts between 80 and 100 minutes. Both brain and body then need a further 20 to 30 minutes to wake up and function at a normal level. If you interrupt this cycle, it can be worse than not having slept at all.

A really good night should have four cycles – roughly eight hours of sleep in total. That's what we humans need to effectively and sufficiently reboot our system. So, if you want to have a nap, make sure you complete a full sleep cycle of two hours. The first half an hour is your light sleep, where you dream and your brain rests, and then you fall into deep sleep, where your body recovers.

If you are in a pinch, there are always power naps too. Commandos, businesspeople and now even pilots in the cockpit – it wasn't allowed previously – often sleep for 20 to 30 minutes maximum. This means they don't fall into deep sleep and therefore don't need the 20–30 minutes of waking time. This is very good for recuperating some energy for the rest of the day, but it does *not* replace real sleep over time. Use the power nap tactically.

One other important thing to remember is age. The older you get, the more your sleep quality deteriorates. For this reason, you have to watch over your sleep like you watch over your health. It is an intrinsic part of your health, after all.

How do we achieve high-quality rest, then? Here are a few tips that work very well for me:

- Don't keep any electronics in the bedroom: no phones, computers or televisions. This is very important!
- Sports and physical activity can dramatically increase the quality of your sleep. You will fall into deep sleep sooner and recuperate faster. Do some *light* physical activity in the evening before you go to sleep – even a 30-minute walk with the dog will help. Anything too heavy will raise your heart rate and temperature, thereby jeopardizing sound sleep.
- Don't do stressful things just before going to bed. Anything like reading company reports or discussing sensitive topics is a recipe for a disastrous night.
- Go to bed at a time that will allow you to get enough sleep. For example, if I go to bed before 11 pm, I know this will allow me to get the necessary eight hours of sleep (plus some time to actually fall asleep) before I need to get up in the morning.
- If you have a partner, go to sleep at the same time as them. This might be a challenge to begin with, but after a while, you'll be in sync and fall asleep together. Too many couples go to bed at different times, thereby disrupting each other's sleep cycle.

I'd say that most people in business don't respect one or more of the above points. Whenever I sin on even one, though, I am guaranteed to have a bad night.

As my daughter, Camille, recalls: "In our home, my room is downstairs and my parents' room is upstairs. I remember as a child my mum and I would often start chatting about our day just before my parents' bedtime and suddenly I'd hear my dad screaming from his room, 'MISH, MISH!'. He was upstairs waiting for her to go to bed with him! Everybody knows it and laughs about it now. They don't take their phones up there, either. So after 10 pm, you just can't reach them."

SUMMING UP WORKING WITH PEOPLE INTERNALLY

Ultimately, with no people, no business – unless you think you can do it all yourself, which you probably can't – can survive by itself. Find the right people and then teach them well, train them well and treat them well. You need their loyalty, to you and to the company. Everybody has to be behind you if you're going to make it.

Remember, though, *you* are the boss. While delegating and sharing responsibilities is imperative, one person should have the definitive say. Being the boss comes with certain expectations, of course, and if you treat your people like assholes, they'll act like assholes and you'll end up an asshole yourself. Make everyone in your business feel comfortable, welcome and involved, and you'll have a decent shot at besting decline.

There is no place for ego. No one crucial to a company has the luxury of one. Learn to have emotional intelligence and empathy, and you'll experience more compromises than conflicts. If we can all do this, we have a great chance at changing the impersonal and harsh climate of business and mastering decline.

EXTERNALLY

The people you interact with outside your company are equally important. Without them, you have no reason to function or exist. Cultivate cordial relationships with them if you want to keep afloat. It's important, though, to know who *not* to consult about your business – many people will try to sell you snake oil. This is one of many reasons it's important to know how to negotiate – the graceful dance that can dictate whether you win or lose.

Who are your *true* stakeholders? Are your shareholders, customers and suppliers team players or do they fight for short-term personal benefit?

'Stakeholder' is a word that's far too often abused in corporate governance. It's sexy window dressing that seeks to please the audience but is really all about short-term, opportunistic business logics.

Fortunately, though, in the new, unfolding 'systemic' world we're soon to enjoy (see the section 'Looking to the future' in Part One), we will be more and more dependent on various new kinds of stakeholder. Together, these will make up a business 'biotope' (a habitat or community around a business). They will all become equally important as traditional stakeholders, while critically contributing to your ecosystem's efficiency.

CUSTOMERS AND SUPPLIERS

Customers and suppliers are crucial contributors.

In a shrinking market suffering from decline, where less knowledge is at your disposal, your supply side might become more important than your customer side. Doing a thorough supplier analysis is paramount. Consider the options and alternatives you do and don't have. For example, including your suppliers in your business strategy might be the way to go in the future.

Our relationships with our main suppliers have proven to be paramount in our survival. This is especially true of the companies The LYCRA Company, which produces the fibre Lycra, and Nurel, which is part of the Spanish family concern Samca and produces most of our nylon. Those bonds, built over generations and based on respect and friendship, have saved the day during COVID-19 and many of the other crises we've been through.

Our long-lasting partnership with the successful underwear company Van de Velde, whose brands are Marie Jo and Prima Donna, is another textbook example of how business should be conducted as a win-win operation. During COVID-19, we stayed open so we could supply them while most of their other suppliers in Europe were closed. The turnover generated on both sides allowed us to survive in these challenging times. A perfect example of symbiosis!

Ensure you also analyse every aspect of your customer base. If it's a business-to-business (B2B)

relationship, ask yourself these questions:
- Are they financially viable?
- Does their product have a future?
- Do they have a plan if the shit hits the fan?
- How do they treat you?
- Do they share your strategy?
- Do they share your views?
- Is there a fit in the mid to long term?
- Are you dependent on a few of them?
- What is the worst-case scenario?
- How would the worst-case scenario affect your business?

Many big fashion groups' relationships with their textile and garment suppliers tend to be imbalanced and one-sided, favouring the big groups. This is completely outdated and ineffective in a fast-changing world. It might work a while longer in Asia, where a more subdued, administrative business model fits better with the relationship forced upon companies by their big American and European customers. But these big customers shouldn't fool themselves: the Asian market will not take this torment and mistreatment for very much longer. As they become economically stronger and more independent, they won't need to, and relationships will change.

LAWYERS AND CONSULTANTS

In a few exceptional cases, using lawyers has been good for us. But on most occasions, we've ended up paying more in lawyers' fees than what we won in a trial or bargain.

So-called coaches and experts are usually only interested in selling you confusion and invoicing juniors at the rate of seniors. The longer they can 'hold you on the line' by complicating things, scaring you and sending you unreadable, supposedly 'legal and expert' contracts, the more they enrich themselves – and the closer you come to the abyss.

You are the expert on your business. It's unlikely that a junior consultant fresh out of university with no damn idea about your products and sector can help you. They are best avoided, unless *absolutely necessary*. Growing markets are a different story, but in the environment that we trade in, exceptional prudence is required when spending *any* money, especially on services with exorbitant fees. So, keep these people far away from you and your business for as long as possible – you cannot afford them anyway!

Unfortunately, the legal system requires the use of lawyers in certain circumstances. But as long as you control every word of what they write and say, you might be lucky and get out of trouble with their help.

CORPORATE GOVERNANCE AND EXTERNAL DIRECTORS

AGMs. Boards. Auditors. Audit committees. Management committees. Remuneration, strategy and surveillance committees. All an absurdly big waste of time in a medium-sized company.

Too many generals, not enough soldiers.

Although creative, experienced external directors who think outside the box could be very valuable to your company, these people are spread very thin. Most of the time, directors who are only vaguely connected to your company, its products and its markets are of no added value in a declining company fighting for survival. Having a nice lunch once a month with a couple of successful external directors might nurture your ego, but it's not going to help you save the day.

A better way of seeking external brainpower is hosting a boot camp or creative seminar for your stakeholders. If it works for your employees, it can work for other interested parties as well.

SUMMING UP WORKING WITH PEOPLE EXTERNALLY

Choose who you do business with wisely. The relationship you have with your suppliers and customers is symbiotic – you all keep each other afloat. With that in mind, having the best and most agreeable relationships with your outside trading partners is in everyone's best interests. If they're going to keep you healthy and vice versa, it's so much easier if you have mutual respect and concerns.

While you might need assistance from specialists, don't expect them to fully understand your industry or your product. Don't see outside experts as a safety net. Instead, make sure your company can function completely independently. If you get into legal trouble, sure, seek help, but take charge – don't let your counsel control the conversation. Work with them closely and guide what they say on your behalf. It's your company after all; if it goes down, you're out on the street and they'll move on to their next client.

No company operates in a vacuum, but that's not to say you shouldn't be extremely cautious about who to include in your business's survival efforts and hopefully its eventual success.

2. PRODUCT

Your product is the very material of your business – especially in textiles, of course. But, whatever your product might be, if you don't have any of it to sell, then there isn't any money to make. Product feeds cashflow; it is the lifeblood of business. Even if you're selling a service, your service is still a product.

You need to know every part of the process that keeps your product in operation. If something goes wrong, you have to know how to find the problem, but also how to fix the problem that you find.

Diversifying your production can be a vital lifeline, but it's hard to get right. Some strike gold, while others dig for years and never find anything of value. As you'll see below, we tried and tried with varying success – although our latest efforts in creating new brands carry the most promise of all our diversification efforts so far. As you'll remember from Part One, a move into new territory has seen us launch a finished garments branch of our enterprise, something we've never done before. Our brands RectoVerso™ and RV-Elite™ are pioneering, high-quality sportswear lines entirely made in Belgium.

My children Mathieu and Camille are making a great success of this breakthrough Liebaert venture. A large part of their strategy is how they use social media, marketing, photography and branding. I've never been a proponent of marketing, as you'll see – but, in the hands of the next generation, I'm seeing that it can be extremely effective. I'm happy to leave the task to them, though. If you don't have the luxury of delegating, you can get some top tips at the end of this section.

PROCESS

When managing decline, it is paramount to have a thorough knowledge of your production process, both from the technical side and from the planning side (i.e. your flow). This is why I trained for ten years across all departments of the company when I was studying – I learned more in this way than from all my years at university put together.

A lot of CEOs spend most of their time concentrating on either sales or product development, leaving the production side to technical engineers and blue-collar employees. However, if you're going to survive, you must challenge yourself to learn new skills and become a multi-faceted business virtuoso. Don't forget, in order to understand your employees, you need to understand their roles through personal experience – in other words, by doing their jobs yourself. Adding extra strings to your bow will give you much greater dynamism and, while delegating is essential, less dependency on your employees.

Additionally, immersing yourself in a neglected part of your business will allow you to map the talent at your disposal – not just by observing personnel in their current roles but by understanding them as individuals more thoroughly too. You *will* discover quick wins and a world of opportunities. You *will* discover skills they possess outside work that could be extremely valuable to you and your business, especially if you're transitioning toward a different model.

It's also paramount that you have a thorough knowledge of your cost price and margin structure. This is especially true when restructuring. This knowledge will assist you in making the right decisions and avoiding the wrong ones.

You should also ask yourself a number of questions here:
- Is your cost price calculation accurate?
- Is it detailed enough?
- Can it be measured against actual performance?
- Are you losing on budget? On standards? On quality? On margins? On waste?
- Are you labour intensive or are you raw materials intensive?
- How high are your energy costs and what will they evolve into over time?
- What are your overheads? Will these evolve too?
- What are your fixed costs and variable costs?
- How much do you need to invest to keep your company up to date?
- How does this investment match up against expected cash flow?
- What are your most profitable products?

- Who are your most profitable clients?
- Is your product unique?
- Can it be copied or duplicated easily?

Ask yourself one final, fundamental question too: can you resize and only produce profitable products? Or are you dependent on volumes at any price to keep the boat afloat? If so, maybe it's time to quit now.

It's also important to consider whether you have benchmarked your various production steps in relation to your competitors. If your competitors are cheaper or better, maybe you should subcontract part of your processes to them.

Conversely, if yours is a very integrated company, where all aspects of the business are exclusively in your hands, the cost of remaining in this spearhead position becomes higher every year. It makes you vulnerable, too. For instance, you could have been overtaken a long time ago by a specialist in a particular field without even knowing it. Remember, the specialist has only one thing – their lifeblood – on which to concentrate their investment and intelligence. You can never compete with that.

Again, be smart, put your ego aside and don't fight a losing battle. Seek help when needed. It's there to be found. Always be one step ahead; invest in processes that add value and divest other activities that are costing more than necessary.

DIVERSIFICATION

Diversification is easy to talk about but very difficult to achieve.

For 20 years I've tried to diversify, including conducting extensive studies and research about possible relocations to Asia. I couldn't find a single solution that would completely fill the gap caused by our melting turnover. There was no Holy Grail, despite us spending a huge amount of money and an even greater amount of time on its pursuit.

To evidence this perhaps rather surprising claim, here is just a small sample from the long list of trials, errors, hopefuls and non-starters we have encountered. Some of them have had moderate success, others have tanked and others look hopeful for the future. They are:

- Our diversification and investment in carbon fibre knitting *failed*.
- Our diversification and investment in rotary and digital printing was a *mild success* that contributed to our survival.
- We conducted a study of potential Asian partnerships and investments. While this was *unfruitful*, we did make a lot of contacts. In hindsight, though, we're very happy we decided against forming any partnerships in Asia. The vast majority of our competitors that did got screwed and went bankrupt.
- Our diversification in garment-making is *starting to bear fruit*. This could certainly be a good leg to stand on in the near future.

- Branding our fabrics as Nanostitch™ and our garments as RectoVerso™ is *showing real promise.* There is even cross-fertilization between the fabrics brand and the garment brand. The reputation of the one helps to sell the other.
- RV-Elite™, our tailor-made compression brand for elite athletes, has *huge potential.*
- Development of our intellectual property (IP) depot platform, Stampy, has been disappointing so far but still *has potential.*
- Our patent on a needle-righting scanner and robot remains a *big question mark.*
- We have developed and patented a 40GG Weftlock machine that can produce unique compression garments for top athletes. This is ongoing and should work. *We're hopeful.*

While this list is by no means exhaustive, it shows how challenging it is to successfully bring new ideas to the market. Our limited success is certainly not for the lack of trying, as you can see. While some of our efforts may have had some impact and show real promise, we've not unearthed any instant fixes, quick wins or Holy Grails. But it has been worth the search. We've found other things along the way.

We've also looked at diversifications outside textiles and used our extensive travel experience to start an exclusive travel agency. We've opened a separate company, Socrates Projects (www.socrates-private-travel.com), which specializes in bespoke holidays for adventurous families like ours. This company is led by Michou and Mathieu. It is still small but has huge potential now that quality of life is becoming paramount in the post-COVID-19 era.

"

*Challenges
are what makes
life interesting
and overcoming
them is what
makes life
meaningful.*

"

– Joshua J. Marine

MARKETING IN A DECLINING ENVIRONMENT

I have always been more inclined to spend money to maintain high product quality rather than (in my view) wasting it on expensive marketing campaigns. I've always believed that if your product quality and service exceed those of your competitors, your product would sell itself. At least in textiles, that used to be true. However, with the growing need to look for cheaper suppliers, most of our clients began to focus on price rather than quality. This meant that we could no longer rely on our hitherto most effective marketing strategy: word of mouth. It was time to adapt. And so, we did.

For many years, our marketing efforts were solely focused on offline marketing techniques. Showing our products at major textile fairs around the world (Salon Interfilière Paris, Techtextil North America, Première Vision, etc.) was our main strategy for a long time. It used to be an efficient way of getting in touch with our existing customers and acquiring new ones. However, with the industry's shift to Asia, garment manufacturers became extremely sensitive to price. After 2010, we realized that acquiring new customers through fairs was an expensive and highly time-consuming endeavour with little to no return. On average we spent €100,000 per year attending those fairs (and a decade previously we had been spending double that amount). In a declining business, however, it is important to only spend money if doing so can improve your short-term sales. Fairs were no longer doing so, so we stopped doing them.

Additionally, being active in a declining B2B market meant that fancy lead-generation tools and software would not be helpful. The solution? Either we needed to find new markets with lower price sensitivity or we had to try to market ourselves in such a way that our customers and other garment manufacturers would understand the added value of our premium fabrics. We did both. With a business in decline, it is crucial to adapt and try out different things – you just cannot sit around and wait. Try different marketing projects simultaneously because you don't know whether, and where, the shit will stick.

THE DIGITAL ERA

With the digital era unfolding, we decided to invest in a new website, email marketing and content marketing. The use of LinkedIn and blog posts is also essential to keep your customers updated on new developments and share company news.

Today these methods are essential commodities in the marketing landscape but ten years ago they represented a major step for us. We had a very limited budget, so we had to be smart and creative. Our digital strategy was built around awareness and educating. We wanted to put the emphasis on the unprecedented innovation and know-how that were embedded in our products. Our new website, for which we created high-value content, showed the industry not only that we were still alive but also that our fabrics were expensive for a reason. We started building awareness about our rich history, know-how and innovation while also showing the ethical and sustainable side of the business.

At that time, sustainability and corporate governance were hot upcoming topics, so we tried to take
advantage of that.

Although we were a B2B company operating in a
very traditional industry, we decided to embrace
the power of social media – an unknown world
for me. My eldest son, Mathieu, who is our marketing and innovation director, convinced me it
could be a powerful tool in conveying our message
without spending any money. Again, this is very
important for a declining business. We set up Instagram and Facebook pages for the business. Our
content strategy was centred around three core
elements: innovation, history and sustainability.
However, our approaches to the two channels
were slightly different. On Instagram we used
more inspirational posts and insider perspectives,
while on Facebook we tried to be more opinion-
ated and provide real-time content (e.g. breaking
news, events and trends). For a declining business,
social media channels are a very cost-efficient way
of marketing your product or service. Make sure
you take advantage of that.

Mathieu made it clear that this strategy was one
for the long run and would not suffice on its own.
The process of delivering a message and creating
awareness with a tight marketing budget takes a
lot of time.

To our surprise, our social media pages generated
more engagement from end consumers rather
than our actual B2B customers. They liked our
story and innovative approach within the 'boring'

textile industry. This presented a new opportunity. What if we were to build awareness among end consumers to make our B2B clients realize their customers care about our story and what our fabrics have to offer?

BUILDING OUR FIRST BRAND

One of my biggest frustrations in dealing with my customers was the fact that they were reluctant to highlight the uniqueness of our fabrics to the end consumer. If you were not involved in the industry, you could not identify whether underwear had been made with Liebaert Textiles fabric or lesser-quality fabric. Our clients did not advertise the two any differently. To know the difference, you had to wear the garment. In other words, the consumer did not know of our existence. I desperately wanted to change that because I knew it would be essential to the factory's survival.

The solution could have been to set up strategic partnerships with some of our biggest clients. Unfortunately, that was never really an option. They simply did not grasp the added value of our fabrics and the need to educate the consumer about it. As a businessman, I understood why they were reluctant. But my moral compass disagreed. I firmly believed they were wrong. I wanted to make our fabrics a household name in the industry and especially among end consumers. In theory, we wanted consumers to choose our customers' garments because they knew the garments were made from our fabrics. Ideally, they would see our name and feel our fabric and instantly think about unprecedented innovation and quality.

With that in mind, Mathieu pitched the idea to build a brand – a brand that encompassed our finest (and most expensive) fabrics. "We could be the Gore-Tex™ of the elastic fabrics," he said. I was hesitant but agreed to the idea, on the condition that it would not exceed our current marketing budget. And so, in 2016, Nanostitch was born. This is a group of premium elastic fabrics that are both lighter and smoother than any other on the market. They were made possible thanks to the unique combination of exclusive micro-threads and custom-made warp knitting machines.

Nanostitch 50GG machine: the finest warp knit machine in the world and a Liebaert specialty.

RV-Elite:
the ultimate
tailor-made
compression
garment for
elite athletes.
(To see this and
other Liebaert
products and
fabrics: www.
liebaert.com)

Mathieu created the Nanostitch brand using simple, cost-efficient techniques:

- Working with a small local branding agency that understood his vision and what their role was in this project
- Involving various people in his network (both inside and outside the business) in a branding workshop

- Creating a separate website, for which he drafted the content himself
- Always keeping the point of view of the customer in mind throughout the process by relying on the sales team's present and past experiences with clients
- Creating the Nanostitch Box – a commercial display box of the fabrics along with all the necessary technical specs that could easily be shown or sent to prospects

The total cost of this branding project was around €70,000.

With the new brand, we decided to take a swing at a new market: sportswear and activewear. Thanks to the high-performance technical specs of these fabrics (quick-drying, sweat-wicking, odour control, etc.), we could prove that they were objectively better than anything else on the market – both in quality and in performance.

With that in mind, Mathieu sent his Nanostitch Boxes to sportswear manufacturers all around the globe. Progress was slow but seeds were being planted. We even got a sit-down with Adidas! Although many of the manufacturers were impressed with both the quality and the technical specs of the fabrics, none of them really converted. As always, price was the issue. On average, a Nanostitch fabric was 30% more expensive than other fabrics from manufacturers' current suppliers. Based on that information, we were doomed to fail – and deep down we had always known that. However, we were able to profile ourselves as an innovative, high-quality textile manufacturer in a new market. Although it was no short-term success, in the long run this endeavour proved to be a door to several new opportunities. For example, today there is a cycling brand made exclusively from Nanostitch fabrics.

The lesson here is that marketing in a declining environment requires a lot of perseverance and flexibility. Some things might not work immediately but could be highly valuable later. Don't lose hope but be ready to let some projects simmer so you can start or finish others in the meantime. Plant various seeds and give them time to grow.

BECOMING A HOUSE OF BRANDS

Closing a multimillion-euro deal with a sportswear giant was not going to happen. The big sportswear manufacturers were just too cost driven. The experience Mathieu and I had with these major players made us realize they would never work with us unless we reduced our prices drastically. For them, price was way more important than quality. I fundamentally disagreed with that philosophy. On that note, we decided to tackle the sportswear market by manufacturing our own garments. It was an entrepreneurial dream of mine to produce a complete finished good. And so, in 2018, we started building our own business-to-consumer (B2C) sportswear brands: RectoVerso and RV-Elite.

Rectoverso: high-quality athleisure wear and 100% made in Belgium.

The idea originated from one of our innovation projects back in 2015. We developed a special fabric that incorporated elastane both in the width and the length, providing consistent and high compression all around. This is perfect for compressive garments. We partnered with the renowned Sport Science Laboratory – Jacques Rogge of Ghent University to initiate a research project on the effect of our compression fabric on athletes. The research required specific garments, such as leggings and shorts, made from the fabric.

Instead of outsourcing, we tried crafting the leggings and shorts ourselves. We bought some sewing machines and an automatic fabric-cutting machine. We rounded up employees who had sewing experience and those willing to learn a new skill. We installed the small sewing department in the old cafeteria of the factory. To my surprise, the quality of the sample leggings and shorts was top notch. The research project was ready to be launched. Unfortunately, though, it would take two full years to yield conclusive results. During that time, we needed to plant another seed and launched our athleisure brand RectoVerso.

MARKETING OUR RECTOVERSO AND RV-ELITE PRODUCTS

Here is some advice based on how we have tackled the marketing of our RectoVerso and RV-Elite products:

- **Have a good story to tell.**
  Make sure your brand has something unique – an attribute, product or message that sticks. With ongoing globalization and digitalization, you have to be able to set your brand apart in order for it to be seen and heard.
- **Know your brand's consumer before building the brand.**
  Once you've drafted the brand's identity, it is time to identify and analyse your target audience. Surveys, personal interviews and focus groups are great ways of getting consumer insights for little money.

- **Positioning is key.**
  Make sure you know what position you want
  your brand to have in the market and how you
  want it to be perceived in the mind of your
  customer. Your marketing strategy should
  stem from that. All your marketing efforts
  should maximize the positioning you want
  your brand to have.
- **Work with freelancers and smaller agencies.**
  Whether it's graphic design, digital marketing,
  web development or other aspects involved in
  building your brand, at some point you will
  need to get help. To keep your budget low,
  you can work with freelancers or smaller
  local agencies that charge lower fees.
- **In B2C, an omnichannel approach wins.**
  Selling through your own e-commerce
  website ensures you have control over
  your margins. However, bringing traffic to
  your website requires a lot of time and
  marketing effort (search engine optimization,
  digital marketing, etc.). Third parties
  are crucial to building short-term brand
  awareness and market insights, but they will
  eat away at your margins. Adopt a healthy mix
  that maximizes your profits but also grows
  your brand. A big, successful customer of
  ours tried a one-channel approach once and
  learned the hard way that caution is a safer
  strategy. After investing millions in direct
  e-commerce, and losing a lot of angry retail
  customers in the process, the company had
  to back-pedal and spend even more time,
  money and effort trying to recuperate
  lost relationships.

- **Take a balanced approach.**
  Beware of extreme, one-sided trends because for every trend there is a counter trend!
- **Hire motivated students.**
  Salary costs in Belgium are among the highest in the world. Over the past three years, we've hired multiple student interns who were looking to gain valuable experience. Most of them will have a certain skill set and will be eager to work. They can be a real asset to your marketing team and won't cost you a penny.
- **Get government funding for your projects.**
  In some countries, such as Belgium, you can apply for certain types of subsidies. Although this may require extra paperwork, it is a good way of financing some of your projects.

All in all, our marketing and branding efforts have kept us afloat and provided a fresh breeze throughout the company. They show both internal and external stakeholders that we are still going. Marketing in a declining landscape is especially difficult because you must cope with extreme budget constraints. There is no way of knowing whether one project is more likely to be successful than another. The key is to try to follow your gut while also listening to the people around you. Don't become reckless and spend everything on one project. You can't afford that. Adopt a balanced approach and analyse each project periodically, and then, based on your analysis, redistribute the available funds.

Some of the most important aspects of marketing in a declining business are creativity, problem-solving skills and resilience within your marketing team. Only a team with those attributes will be able to thrive in a declining environment.

CREATIVITY

Lateral thinking and creativity are powerful weapons in difficult situations. I've been making use of them my whole career thanks to a voluntary course I took at university, called 'Creative Problem-Solving.' I thought that this introductory course would greatly complement my main subject of applied economics.

The course was not on the University of Antwerp's academic programme, but the subject intrigued me. So, I took it. Every Wednesday afternoon for 15 weeks, Professor De Bruyn guided my classmates and me through the basics of solving problems in a far more effective way than I'd experienced before. His way is an underused approach known by too few people.

Professor De Bruyn was both an extraordinary storyteller and a very passionate teacher. His course orbited around the teachings of two masters in this field – Alex Osborn and Edward de Bono – looking at Osborn's *Applied Imagination* and de Bono's *Lateral Thinking*.

In their texts, these two thinkers explain how we can connect the right side of our brain (emotional) with the left side (logical) and change our thinking patterns. The logical brain (on the left) has by far the upper hand in our daily lives. So, we have to train it to ignore its instinctive thinking habits and venture beyond reason. The aim is to break out of the box. Our left brain quickly puts up logical walls and excludes a lot of solutions because they don't seem logical. But maybe logic isn't the only thing that works.

In the course, we were taught how to break these logical patterns. To do so, we needed to recognize that such patterns can be based on preconceived ideas that are often, in reality, wrong. Therefore, some of the solutions we exclude could be very useful in getting us out of whichever dark hole in which we're currently stuck.

After the introductory course, I decided to take a full one-year expert course at De Bruyn's own Center for the Development of Creative Thinking. There I was surrounded by businesspeople, most of whom were Dutch, who had an open, free mentality and therefore were well suited to this training.

We did real-life exercises based on various companies, and we all had to write a thesis developing new methods for applying lateral thinking. I developed a creative brainstorm process based on images and senses rather than words, and this proved to be very useful in an international environment where participants speak different languages. Once we had achieved our degree, we could teach other scholars.

These lessons from lateral thinking have helped me shift my thought patterns when I've been faced with issues that I thought at first sight were unsolvable. In fact, I've implemented this training routinely in my own company over the past three decades. My introductory course to creative problem-solving is an exhausting three days, but the results are spectacular every time.

We usually come out with between 200 and 250 new ideas, of which at least a dozen can be implemented right away. These are 'quick wins.'

Here is an example: we organized a short brainstorm to find a name for our athleisure brand and found we were stuck in our thinking patterns, as we couldn't find a consensus and choose between all the names that came out. I organized a game as a break and during that game we showed a garment that was sewn inside out. Then suddenly somebody shouted "Recto Verso" (a French term that means 'double-sided') and that's how we got out of our mental blockage.

This is the strength of these techniques: they artificially create a 'eureka' moment, as with Archimedes in his bath (he suddenly came to see water as a measurement instrument in addition to a washing tool). Of course, these techniques need training and a lot of practice.

Explaining all the brain-training techniques that lateral thinking encompasses would take too long. The most important thing to remember is that you must be in the right frame of mind before participating in a creative problem-solving session. This crucial mindset is called creative mental attitude (CMA).

Here are the 'rules' that define it:
- Suspend judgment
- Allow people to say things that twist or bend reality, as in a role play, which is basically the essence of a creative session
- 'Stupid ideas' get special attention
- Respect everyone's privacy
  – no personal comments
- Hitch-hike on everybody else's ideas
- Remain humble
- Break patterns
  – look for preconceptions
- Freewheel around random themes
  – some 'fun' moments unstick our thinking patterns
- Quantity breeds quality (the more ideas, the better)
- The group owns all the ideas
  – no individual credit

Having about eight to ten people per group is ideal. One third should be specialists, another third should be generalists and the final third should be 'wild geese.' The wild geese usually offer the most potential for lateral thinking, especially children from the age of 12 onwards. They are blank canvases with very few preconceptions and quick, agile brains. Being able to jump from one terrain to another is hugely useful – something they do with no issue.

I would warmly encourage any manager confronted with a seemingly unsolvable problem, in any business climate but especially one in decline, to take the time to reinvent their mindset and host one of these sessions. It is a genuinely therapeutic exercise!

SUMMING UP PRODUCT

Know your product. Know your process. It's pretty much as simple as that. If you're not the expert in what you make, why should anyone buy it from you? Knowledge breeds confidence, which in turn breeds creditworthiness.

That's not to say get complacent – be brave and expand your range if the right idea comes along. Always be prepared to learn more and try new things. As long as your staple product and production are cast iron, you have the freedom to explore.

Ultimately, your creativity might be what saves you. If you're not prepared to improvise and move with the changes in society, your products will most likely be forgotten and committed to a quickly fading past.

3. STRUCTURE

Poor structures don't stand up to strong winds. If you haven't put much thought into your structure, or it's bloated and over-encumbered, it will hold together during the good times. However, if the climate changes, your company will fall apart.

What keeps a structure safe in the face of adversity is *flexibility*. Build flexibility into both the horizontal and vertical axes of your business and you'll be indestructible.

Decide whether you want to be integrated or work with subcontractors. While there were once great virtues in integration, a disintegrated company can enjoy more flexibility and better evade disasters in harsh conditions. I would recommend a network of collaborating forces as more appropriate for today's business environment.

HORIZONTAL VERSUS VERTICAL FLEXIBILITY

Having flexibility in your organization's structure will ensure you get the best results in the shortest possible time. Having workers who possess multiple skills on the horizontal axis, complemented by managers who can operate flexibly on the vertical axis, will save you a lot of cost and the time it takes to restructure, while also keeping your most valuable players in action.

As Kevin, our COO, says: "We have a very flat structure. I know a lot of people in companies of all sizes; I've never heard of anywhere else with such a horizontal structure. It gives people the chance to think alongside management and the boss and the company. If people have ideas, we listen. This creates the feeling that this is indeed also their company. That's why these people have been very flexible in difficult times."

HORIZONTAL

In total, we have about 20 departments in our factory, each one demanding its own unique skill-set. To ensure we have the multiskilled horizontal axis so crucial to maintaining profit in a declining industry, we have trained about 30% of our staff in two or three different departments over the past five years.

We could not have foreseen how valuable this exercise would be come the arrival of the COVID-19 crisis. Having employees who could flex their expertise and skills allowed us to innovate and make masks, boosting production from 0% to 100% in a short space of time.

Despite the strength of Belgian unions and totally rigid social laws, we managed to organize the multiskilled environment necessary to boost production during the pandemic crisis. This was overwhelmingly thanks to our amazing workforce,

who were on board immediately without any per-
suasion on our part. In fact, they volunteered.

So, not only did we manage to cut our losses by
selling face masks, but we were also able to protect
our workers' jobs with their own inbuilt flexibility:
definitely a win-win situation. These people are
team players, ones who are becoming ever more
invaluable to the company and who will have
secure jobs at Liebaert's until my last breath.

On top of that, it makes their professional life a lot
more interesting as they can shift from one job to
another and thus fight the monotony that infects
a lot of staff members.

VERTICAL

My first boss always told me that if we could train
people to be vertically flexible in our organization,
we could build the strongest company in the world.

If managers and executives can do administrative
and secretarial work, and if engineers can do technical and unskilled labour once in a while, through
their dynamism it is possible to correct all of an
organization's little kinks and flaws. Not only will
this dramatically enhance communication and
motivation, but pockets of frustration will also be
ironed out and many improvements can be made
quickly and diligently.

During COVID-19, all of our managers have had
to do the jobs of their subordinates; they led by
example and were able to understand their team's
frustrations. This streamlined our systems' flow

and comprehensively boosted our organization's efficiency all round.

The big lesson here is that the *only* way to improve subordinates' jobs is by doing them yourself for a while and understanding the issues they face.

But let's not forget the flipside of the coin: giving your workforce the responsibilities of their managers helps them to understand and appreciate the dark side that comes with privileges of seniority. They can then see that their leaders' lives aren't actually that easy and consequently their understanding of the company improves drastically.

On top of that, this method allows you to screen those workers who have management potential. This might sound implausibly utopic, but 50% of our company's managers are former factory workers.

Without this 'musical chair philosophy,' they would never have even had the opportunity.

INTEGRATION VERSUS SUBCONTRACTING

History shows that both integration and subcontracting can work, but often companies get the timing wrong. With that in mind, keep a close eye on world economics and geopolitical evolutions – these observations will tell you what you should do and when.

A few decades ago, for instance, it made a lot of sense to integrate a critical mass in one company. However, in the current climate, I would strongly recommend working with teams of efficient sub-contractors who are experts in their field, and focusing on your own specific expertise. Having these satellite assistants is the best way to maximize your strengths.

At Liebaert, for example, we decided to concentrate on beam dyeing and lost our expertise in jet dyeing over the years. However, as our fabrics are becoming finer and lighter and have a very high Lycra content, jet dyeing is often the better process from a quality point of view.

Instead of investing heavily in machinery that we were not sure we would master properly, we looked throughout Europe and found a good partner. As commission-based (subcontracting) textile dyeing is a disappearing industry, we helped this partner to increase their offering. As a result, our quality is 50% better than when we try to do it ourselves on our beam dyeing machines. Another win-win relationship!

Concerning rotary printing, on the other hand, as the industry was also disappearing, we decided to invest ourselves and be totally independent of our ailing subcontractors. Although we were previously not anywhere approaching masters in this technique, we became specialists within a couple of years and our quality was a lot better than what our previous partners were delivering. This is now one of our most successful departments.

So, as you can see, there is no black-and-white answer. Careful consideration should be made before opting for one approach or the other.

RESTRUCTURING DOS AND DON'TS

On restructuring at Liebaert, Kevin says: "Any downsizing or restructuring has been prepared half a year or a year in advance. Every time, we'd communicate honestly and transparently about what we were going to do. The policy is 'fair, but firm.' Firm doesn't leave much room for any unnecessary discussion, but fair helps to keep people on side. Most of the people who sadly had to leave the company knew the situation and knew that we wouldn't be downsizing if it wasn't completely necessary."

Restructuring a company is like a game of chess. It requires careful planning and starts long before the actual action takes place. I would recommend starting to plan at least six months in advance, but preferably one year.

It's crucial to remember, too, that you should always restructure when you still have the cash to do it and can still afford the expense. Stay ahead of the game and take the time to think deeply about your choices and decisions. Be aware that a last-minute, knee-jerk restructuring to save a sinking ship is bound for failure.

Be patient. You *must* be patient. Do your preparations long in advance and study many different scenarios that involve a variety of approaches to cost-cutting and how much to cut.

Restructure the most expensive parts first. Don't be fooled into thinking it's always personnel costs that you can scrap. It could be energy, overheads, marketing, maintenance, or sales offices and fairs. Often it's the company overall – meaning, for example, your company is too big for its current level of production.

Once you've devised your restructuring pro-gramme, *communicate, communicate, communicate!* You should do this inside and outside the company, to all workers, managers, shareholders, suppliers and customers – anyone with a vested interest of any kind in your success.

If you have a good relationship with your per-sonnel and they are fully aware of the situation, the planned restructuring will become evident to them long before it starts. Remember, they are not stupid. They will realize *something* has to happen to save the company. So, keep them in the loop. They don't need to know every single detail, but don't shut them out. They'll appreci-ate it and respect you, and not to mention morale will be higher because they will feel involved and respected too.

From a financial point of view, perhaps the best option is to restructure in phases over a longer period. Be aware, though, that while this can save costs, it's a dangerous game. Restructuring has an adverse effect on people's mood, and therefore their attitude, which in turn leads to worse service and suffering quality. So, if you have the means to do so, I'd recommend taking a short and decisive in-depth approach: it's expensive but, if you can afford it, worth it.

As soon as the law permits, warn your customers and suppliers. This is a must. Always warn them; otherwise, they might hear about the restructuring from elsewhere – a third party or, worse, the press – and get very nervous.

If unions are involved, use the stick-and-carrot method. Start with the worst-case scenario. In the end, and usually after serious negotiations, you have to give them something. But don't make it too easy for them. They still have to convince their members that they've 'won' *something*. So be prepared to talk about closing the company as a serious alternative if the unions don't go along with your wishes.

NEGOTIATING

You're going to have to know how to negotiate, and negotiate *well*, if you're undertaking a period of restructuring. So, here are some bite-sized tips:

- **Be courageous but not reckless.**
- **Know when to be bold.**
  Sometimes you have to play the bluff as in poker and threaten with devastating consequences if the other party is not playing along. When you restructure the strong ace up your sleeve toward unions and governing authorities is the closing of the complete company with a social bloodbath as a consequence. This can be very

efficient but could backfire if used too often or with the wrong timing. Loosing credibility in negotiations is the worst outcome one can wish.

- **Go rested.**
(see the section above on the importance of rest).

- **Remain calm.**
If you are too emotional about the issue, send a trusted and well-briefed colleague onto the stage in your place. Staying behind the curtain, ready to advise, gives your negotiator an excuse to stall and allows them time to think. This technique is very efficient if you have to deal with emotional issues where the parties are so biased and emotionally involved that a direct confrontation would lead to a battle of egos and a stalemate. We once had to negotiate two small restructures with the labour unions, and they are definitely not little kitties to deal with, especially if the boss is in front of them. This is why Kevin (our COO) did all the negotiations alone. This took the emotional side out of the equation. Whenever a blockage occurred, Kevin could play the clock and say that he had to consult with me before moving on. The same happened when we negotiated the buy-out of my cousin. There was no way we could sit at the same table and find a compromise. So my son Mathieu negotiated alone and an agreement was reached quite swiftly.

- **Negotiate a solution quickly.**
Do not let the problem turn into a cancer. Use your negotiator (the person who allows you to stay behind the curtain) efficiently. But don't use them to bring things to a standstill.

Throughout the whole process, ensure that you keep communicating with all the people who are involved – this includes management, workers and unions. There may be legal restrictions about what you can say to whom, but know your options and communicate as much as you can within them. Everyone will sleep better.

Like I've said elsewhere, when restructuring, start from the top (management) and work your way down to the bottom (workers). Prioritize attitude over knowledge – keeping the people who know the most but do the least won't help your company. Don't keep people because of their job title, either. If you can afford to, remove career seniority from consideration. This might be expensive, but you don't want to be left with an unmotivated old people's home. *Choose the doers.* Choose those who are motivated and ready to help you defeat decline. Fortunately, the older workforce often has the best attitude anyway. So, this is not often a particularly big issue.

It's also important to be prepared for compromises. They can help to maintain good relations with both your personnel and the unions. Be diplomatic and treat everyone as well as possible. You want them on your side. If you leave a bloody battlefield behind with a lot of grudges and frustration, there is no way your company will survive.

Once your restructuring is done, make sure the remaining stakeholders, such as personnel, unions, customers and suppliers, are appeased and feel positive about the future. As soon as the company is doing better, start hiring a younger team. This sends a very strong message both internally and externally.

> *"Hire character, train skills."*

Peter Schutz

TAKING ON THE CHALLENGE OF RESTRUCTURING

Here are some tips that have stood me in good stead when it comes to restructuring:

- Prepare yourself like an athlete for a marathon
- Surround yourself with trustworthy people
- Prepare long in advance
- Cash is king
- Learn everything about your products, production, suppliers, customers, costs, price margins and legal conditions
- Be transparent with your team and teach them to be flexible
- Restructure from the top down
- Don't count on outsiders to bail you out: you are on your own
- Keep a healthy work–life balance

SUMMING UP STRUCTURE

Your structure should adapt over time to the conditions it finds itself in. If that's not possible, you are unlikely to survive. Flexibility is critical, and you can secure it by having multi-functional employees who can perform numerous roles at different levels. Ultimately, your company's structure is how you've organized your people. You can only find out what works best structurally if you're in constant communication with the people in your company. Discuss with them what works, and then implement it.

4. MONEY

In a declining company, your money situation is difficult but also relatively simple, because you can't afford anything. Essentially, your financial mantra should be: have cash, invest cautiously and avoid banks. That might sound counter-intuitive, but you need to stand up on your own. If you're prepared for anything, you should be fine.

CASH

Cash is king. Cash is the key. Cash gives you options. No cash means no options. In this position, you're dependent on others to determine your strategy. You don't want that. Therefore, squirrel cash away long before you really need it. Take debt while you're profitable, even if you don't need the money – it could be your future saving grace. Remember the starting premises at the beginning of this part of the book: prepare for all likely eventualities.

Always generate cash flow. If you feel that your cash flow is going to be negative for a period of six months or longer, consider either closing your company or dramatically reorganizing it. If this is done in time, you might even be able to get some cash out for shareholders.

INVESTMENTS

Investing is a one-way practice. It consumes cash. If you change your mind, most of the time you cannot get rid of what you've invested in without a big penalty.

However, any investment that saves you money, time or both is worth looking at. But always frame your decisions with the basic maxim of a declining company: how long will it take you to be paid back? Anything longer than three years should be questioned, and anything over five years should be forgotten.

Make sure, also, to have a clear understanding of what maintaining your old machines and equipment costs. If you are considering a new investment, assess whether the purchase is flexible – in other words, is it versatile such that it can be used for something other than the original reason you bought it?

You always have the option to buy second-hand as well. Finding a reputable supplier of second-hand machines could be a canny strategy for investing in new machinery without paying more than necessary.

But always make sure you have enough cash to keep your production up to date and in pristine condition. There is no way you will last with an outdated and poorly maintained factory. Keeping your buildings and amenities in good condition is also paramount for your image within and outside the company.

BANKS AND CREDIT

My grandfather was the Belgian Minister of Finance for six years. He knew what he was talking about and always warned me: "Banks give you an umbrella when it's not raining. When it gets wet, they take the umbrella away."

At the beginning of the COVID-19 crisis, the financial world was swamped with an endless amount of cheap cash. I knew that this cash was going to be funnelled in creative ways to the stock exchange, destined to be used for speculation, instead of going to the high street to boost confidence and restart the economic engine through consumption.

After many months of interruption, Wall Street and Main Street have never been further apart. We are creating a *huge* speculation bubble that will explode in the coming years. I'm sure of it. Watch.

Banks and governments are pumping millions into loss-making biotech companies, apps and tech start-ups in the hope that they will lay a golden egg someday. These highly speculative investments are like playing roulette – except these people are doing it with taxpayers' money. Your money. My money.

I am *not* in favour of artificially supporting lame ducks, but I would rather give a fighting chance to a manufacturing company employing hundreds of people than invest in an IT business employing two nerds developing an app to change water into gold. As I alluded in the premises at the start of this part of the book, achieving alchemy is exceptionally rare – the visionary billionaires, the Elons and the Zucks are few and far between.

Here is a beautiful example of how the banks reacted to COVID-19. Our company had no debts; it was cash positive, having made profits for the past 30 years, except for the most recent year, 2019. During 2020, we made profits again, actually helping to produce masks upon our city mayor's request, and the situation was under control. When our 2019 balance sheet was published showing a loss, one of our house banks called us to cancel our credit line. We had been a customer of this bank for 100 years!

Both our CFO and I went completely ballistic because we had €1 million cash in our bank account, we hadn't asked for a loan and we weren't even asked to explain the previous year's bad results.

Can you imagine what their reaction would have been if we were *really* in trouble?! Remember: *banks offer you an umbrella only when it's not raining.*

The only leverage you can have with a bank is if you're deeply indebted to them and they're afraid to lose their stake if they withdraw their support. A very recent US president might be someone to ask about that situation. But not me. This is a very uncomfortable position for both parties, and it usually presages bankruptcy.

Basically, do not count on banks – you are on your own. Learn to live with it!

5. EVALUATION

There's a well-known phrase in French, 'les finances sont les nerfs de la guerre.' Essentially, the translation means, 'finances are the nerves of war.' But what is the deeper meaning of this rather poetic expression? In a human body, the nerves connect the brain, the spinal cord, the muscles and the organs. They are present everywhere. Without them, the body couldn't function at all, and if they are disrupted or disturbed, things begin to go wrong very quickly. Similarly, in a war or in a company, if your finances aren't the very network that holds everything together, that ensures one organ communicates healthily with another, you're dead and defeated – your chances of victory are slim.

Know your numbers. All of them. And don't expect someone else to do it for you.

In my honest opinion, if you have the guts and ego to manage a company, the least you can do is understand and control the numbers at your business's core. Leaving this task to bookkeepers, CFOs, auditors and controllers is equivalent to asking the ship's engineer to steer the ship through a storm.

Before you decide whether to continue, close or sell – your three realistic options – the first thing you need to know is the value of your declining business. Consider:

- The net asset value (NAV)
- The closing value – this is the NAV minus the cost of retrenchment (social liabilities) and a very critical and conservative assessment of your inventory
- Your company's cash flow or profitability value going forward

I would say that a cash flow multiplicator of five or a net profit multiplicator of ten is the maximum you will get for your declining company based on the current numbers or the numbers after a thorough, well-organized and well-documented reorganization proposal. Usually an average of the NAV and a cash flow multiple is the fairest way to evaluate a declining company, although evaluating the cash flow going forward remains a toss of a coin.

Let's now take a close look at how we can calculate the NAV of a company, as well as at the pitfalls hidden behind every line in our balance sheet and profit-and-loss (P&L) accounts.

I realize that there are many more 'academic' and complex ways of evaluating a company, but I have tried to keep the process as simple and understandable as possible. Doing so has worked for me up to now.

ASSETS

Your assets are your primary source of value. They could be your properties, your stock, your investments, your customers, or even something intangible and intellectual like your brand. These immaterial assets are growing in significance and should be recognized alongside traditional quantifiers of value.

GOODWILL AND IMMATERIAL ASSETS SUCH AS PATENTS AND BRANDS

I don't dispute that there can be real value in these particular types of assets. However, often, they are simply bookkeeping hocus pocus that beefs up the value of a company or enriches a few shareholders. In a declining company, don't count on getting anything for or from these assets.

If you have a very strong and long-established brand or unique patents, they might be worth something to a particular investor, but such situations are exceptions rather than the rule.

However, the emotional value of your company – a concept developed in the triple accounting philosophy of Professor Michel 'Mike' de Kemmeter (see the Introduction) – might be worth factoring into your considerations. Values in business are certainly changing, and now ethics, sustainability, history, social responsibility and cohesion are gaining prominence, as are the innate qualities of your employees: their happiness, mentality, skills, experience and capital. Soon enough, these factors may be *the* way to value companies – if this new economy we're discussing is fully realized.

These details come into play once you have decided to continue running your company and are already working out a 'new self' for your business.

FIXED ASSETS

With fixed assets, you should only consider their resale (second-hand) value. If you've been a 'safe' businessperson and undervalued your assets, some profits could be hiding here. However, make sure you seek an *expert* assessment of their real value.

FINANCIAL ASSETS: PARTICIPATIONS

You should evaluate your financial participations' value in the same way as your fixed assets. Exercise very critical judgment. You might be surprised by how many hidden losses suddenly appear.

There is one essential question to remember, too: can you easily sell your participations? If the answer is no, then their value shouldn't be a penny more than their equity value.

FINANCES

If your finances are in cash, this is a reasonably straightforward assessment. But if they are not liquid and are instead based on complicated and risky investments, you might end up with no value at all. So, again, be very critical! In declining environments, cautious, conservative judgments are much more appropriate than optimistic, overconfident ones. Establishing this attitude should save you some nasty shocks.

CUSTOMERS

Look at all your open invoices. Are these customers going to pay you? How long does it take them to pay? Are they healthy? In your sector, probably not!

Study their balance sheets and evaluate whether they even have the capacity to pay you. You'd be surprised. This research could result in a very sour pill to swallow, but it's better to do it as soon as possible and get the pain out of the way and your hands firmly on the reins.

Credit insurance can be a helpful relief, but in my experience, nobody will insure customers in high-risk declining markets.

So, in a nutshell, being realistic, you might have to write off a lot of these dues and debts, thus reducing your overall value assessment.

INVENTORIES

If you've been a safe and responsible manager, your inventories will be correctly valued. However, in a declining market, as most inventories are linked to future sales to a particular customer, the risk is high.

If you have far fewer customers than you did before, consider that part of your inventory might never be sold – or, if you're lucky, only with a significant discount.

Evaluating every single product in your inventory can be an eye-opener. Doing so might even tell you which of the three available options to choose: continue, close or sell.

SUMMING UP ASSETS

Regularly assess your assets. The areas listed above are not completely exhaustive, of course – you may have another type of asset in your company. But whatever individual parts make up your net value, know their worth inside out, back to front and upside down. Without a clear picture of your value, you're shooting in the twilight.

LIABILITIES

If assets are your main source of value, your liabilities will tell you where you got the money to create this value.

CAPITAL AND RESERVES

Consider this line frozen and lost forever – certainly if you see no end to the decline. There is *no way* you'll be able to pay yourself dividends during major losses and decline.

At Liebaert, for example, we kept all profits in the company during the good years, thereby creating a large amount of financial reserves and making us independent of banks. These reserves were kept in the company and when the tide turned, they gave us the necessary financial strength to weather the storm. This buffer, however, is money that will stay on your books as long as the company is in dodgy waters.

This line is your life insurance for negotiations with banks, suppliers and customers. It gives them the necessary confidence and reassurance to keep supporting you in difficult times. It also shows how much capital your shareholders have left in the company over the years. This is the profit that shareholders have decided not to pay out over the years and left as cash reserves in the company.

LONG-TERM DEBT

Only approach this option if you *know* you can pay the interest and there are no guarantees on assets. Having debt could well be a good pressure point to keep the banks on board. But be very careful: I wouldn't recommend debts above half your capital and reserves, depending on cash flow. Make sure, as well, that you have a sensible repayment schedule, of course.

SHORT-TERM DEBT AND OTHER REGULATORY DEBTS (SOCIAL SECURITY, VAT AND TAXES)

Consider all debts of this kind owed. There is no bargaining leverage possible. If you have to start debasing yourself to postpone repayments, you're already dead without knowing it yet.

SUPPLIERS

You honour your debts, full stop! If you cannot pay your suppliers, in my view, you are bankrupt. Game over! Time to shut down shop.

Never put yourself in that position. Honour your suppliers. If you want to survive, keep them as friends. You might need them as much as they need you! In fact, you might need them more. Don't forget, though, that most of them will be dealing with the same carnage as you are anyway, thanks to the decline. So be extra-vigilant and don't harm them even more.

SUMMING UP LIABILITIES

Some liabilities are necessary and expected, while others only manifest if you choose to buy into them. Long-term debt has to be balanced with solid capital and reserves.

PROFIT AND LOSS

This is your scoresheet. Keep a clean sheet and you're home and dry. Let's go through both parts: income and costs.

INCOME

Know your cost price structure by heart. It's essential that you're on top of the numbers. Know your average price, too. And know your margins on each product, by heart – seriously. You'll be grateful for it.

Closely evaluate your cost base and your budgets. Ask yourself a few questions:
- Are you losing on budgets?
- On margins?
- On average pricing?
- How much is your wage bill as a percentage of your income?
- What are your overheads?
- Can you afford them?
  (If not, restructure from the top down
  – see Part Two, Section 3)

- How are your customers, markets and products divided?
- Are you dependent on a few customers, markets or products?

Know the answers to these questions like your survival depends on it. Because it does.

Maybe one of these areas is dominating your company without you even realizing it. Being too dependent on any one of them might be a reason to quit. Because if you're in this position, you're basically putting yourself in a corner and reducing the options available to you.

COSTS

Be completely on top of all your costs. As a principle, weed out any unnecessary ones, starting with the ones that consume the highest percentage.

Find ways to reduce essential costs, if you can: your energy supply, for instance. Gas versus electricity – which one is cheaper? Can you buy a long-term contract? Which one is most suitable for you? Make sure to have a good look around for the best supplier. But never compromise on quality!

A lot of European textile factories rely on a low-cost supply base. At Liebaert, each time we tried this route, our quality and service suffered and it became a logistical nightmare. We don't have the luxury to provide either bad quality or bad service, so we decided to stay with a European supply base. This saved the day when COVID-19 came around. Changing to Asian raw materials would have saved us only 10% – definitely not worth the risk!

Consider your IT costs, too. You can save money by keeping what you have. But definitely invest if implementing new equipment would lead to a direct win.

Our biggest cost at Liebaert is personnel. On average, a factory worker costs €45,000 per year and middle-management costs €70,000 per year. Managers double that amount at least.

Laying people off in Belgium costs one month of salary per working year, so if you have a very loyal and old workforce, as Liebaert does, restructuring costs a fortune. This is what the unions negotiated in the early days with our socialist government. A couple of years ago, we had to lay off 20 factory workers and five from middle management, and it cost us €900,000.

You will easily comprehend, then, that most Belgian companies that are in difficult financial situations simply cannot afford a big restructure. Many have no option other than to file for bankruptcy, thereby creating an even bigger social bloodbath than restructuring might have created.

This is definitely the flip side of Belgian socialism.

In summary, then, only hire when really needed, and restructure when you have the money to do so – in other words, sooner rather than later.

6. OUTSIDE FORCES

Your company is not an isolated ecosystem, no matter its size or structure. There are obligations to the outside world that will come calling on a regular basis. It's best for you to know what they are and how to answer their demands. This comes from obsessive homework and complete awareness. Keep on top of cultural expectations, legal regulations and what your government can do for you.

SUSTAINABILITY

Sustainability has become a very sexy concept, but unfortunately it is also one of the most abused in business. In the vast majority of cases, it's a hollow word used by opportunists for marketing goals. Do we actually know what sustainability stands for? It could be using recycled or biological materials, using renewable energy, having efficient production processes, controlling your supply chain and therefore working environment and wages, or just making sure your business survives and your employees can keep their jobs. This is just the tip of the iceberg, as sustainability comes in so many forms that every company in the world is sustainable in one way or another (and will say so in their marketing), yet none of them really are.

Although at Liebaert we will never claim to be 100% sustainable and we realize we still have a long way to go, sustainability has never been something we do 'on top.' We are intrinsically sustainable. This is partly because of European and Belgian legislation, and partly because of our DNA. The following sections explain our efforts and the corresponding pitfalls.

FAIR WAGES AND WORK ENVIRONMENT

I believe wages and work environment are together one of the biggest challenges facing the fashion industry nowadays. Stories of child labour, collapsing factories, unbearable working conditions and low wages are the rule rather than the exception.

At Liebaert, our European–Belgian system rightly enforces fair wages and a good working environment, so this one is pretty straightforward for us. Or is it? Throughout our history (and even more so currently), we have definitely been tempted by the benefits of producing abroad. Asia, Western Europe and Portugal were all within our reach.

So, is it that bad to produce abroad? Should everything come back to Europe? No, I don't think that is the solution. First of all, this would mean a lot of people already living in poverty would lose their jobs. Secondly, I believe other countries are more specialized than us – for example, in garment-making. Thirdly, it is just too expensive to produce in Belgium. If you're starting up a brand, I would definitely not recommend it. We are lucky we can do it internally because we are vertically integrated and we can afford it.

I think the solution lies in controlling more of your supply chain and enforcing rules. If you're producing abroad, I would recommend doing a thorough analysis of your partner.

FIGHTING MASS CONSUMPTION

This is the most difficult yet the most important aspect of sustainability. Curtailing mass consumption would resolve a huge number of the environmental and societal challenges we face today. In theory, every company that produces non-vital consumption goods is intrinsically unsustainable – us included. But, then again, we need consumption in order to enable businesses to survive, in order to pay taxes and in order to keep people employed – not to forget the positive psychological aspect of consuming. In short, in order to sustain our current societal model (based on capitalism), we need the money. Quite a paradox, right? For me, this is one of the biggest challenges for the future of society, and I currently don't have an answer to it.

At Liebaert, I believe we contribute to fighting mass consumption in several ways. First of all, we produce high-quality fabrics and garments, which means consumers can use them for longer before they wear out. Secondly, our prices are on the high side. This usually means that people won't impulse buy. We see this in relation to our brand RectoVerso – our customers really make thorough buying decisions. The same is true for our fabrics and trims. Thirdly, in our marketing and sales, we don't lure people into impulse buying. We rarely do sales, we have a long-term exchange policy and we are even second-guessing our digital advertising strategy. We don't want you to regret your purchase and have our clothing collect dust in your closet – we want you to wear it until its threadbare. And what happens then? Let's talk about that in the following paragraphs.

RECYCLING AND REUSE

In the textiles business, I believe recycling is one of the most distorted and misunderstood topics out there. It is a very noble cause that could resolve a lot of problems. However, we know the pitfalls behind working with recycled yarns in a way that consumers don't. Maybe our competitors are doing a better job than us, but we've found it a lot more complicated to ensure quality when using recycled yarns. This results in a lot of second-choice fabrics, and a lot more water and energy usage. So, in the long run, the environmental impact is higher.

Furthermore, we're quite sceptical about the recycled materials used in the yarns we purchase. Our yarn suppliers use waste from their initial production process to make their recycled yarns. However, they've now concluded that the demand is so high for their recycled yarns that they don't generate *enough* waste from their regular process. Yet reducing waste was for a long time one of their main 'sustainable' objectives. Another paradox.

Even worse, we've heard of companies producing bottles made with polyethylene terephthalate (PET) solely to be used as recycled material for yarn-making – how misleading is that?

Clothing and fabrics made of certain yarn types cannot be recycled (for now). You can't unravel some clothing, decompose it or reuse its yarn. The only thing you can do with clothing is reuse it. At Liebaert we have a lot of organizations, schools, students and small businesses reusing our second-choice fabrics and leftovers. For RectoVerso, an interesting alternative is the second-hand market. I believe this has huge potential for the future. At RectoVerso, we are still a bit too young to consider this, but we see a lot of successful initiatives where brands have their own second-hand programme.

CONTROL YOUR ECOLOGICAL FOOTPRINT

Liebaert strives to do more than what the strict environmental legislation in Europe and Belgium requires. We call one of my employees the 'Green Man.' He ensures our production process meets the highest standards to minimize our ecological footprint. He has presented me with details of all the certificates we could possibly obtain regarding sustainability and not once have I refused to go through the certification process. Please note that this is a big investment – obtaining these certificates entails not only a financial cost but also a lot of time. However, I believe it is worth it for a growing business because it forces you to evaluate your processes continuously.

THE PARADOX OF 'SUSTAINABILITY'

The hypocrisy of our Western so-called sustainable mindset is clear. So far in this century, we have rightfully fought for the rights of our workers, and this has resulted in fairer wages, a huge social security network and good working conditions. We have rightfully fought for strict laws concerning energy and the environment. The result? Producing in Europe has become so expensive that a large amount – perhaps 50% – of production (especially in textiles and fashion) has moved outside Europe. The hypocrisy? The people fighting for our workers' rights and the environment in Europe are very likely to be queuing at the latest opening of a Primark or H&M store.

We play by the rules, yet the big brands just find their way around them. It is kind of like how all the competitors rode the Tour de France while doping in the 1970s – why would you be the only one not doing it? So, can we blame the big fast-fashion brands? Well, not really. Drastically changing their business model would be the same as committing suicide – they just can't afford to do that.

SUMMING UP SUSTAINABILITY

So, what do we do as a business to get out of this situation? Informing customers is a major part of it. We organize visits to our factory and we arrange a three-day customer training seminar each year, which is probably the best marketing idea we ever had. Even though it doesn't generate direct sales, we believe it is really important to 'preach.' Sustainability shouldn't be used primarily as a marketing tool – it should be your reason for existence. It is about wanting to contribute to a better world.

RULES AND REGULATIONS

Managing a declining company requires a complete set of skills. You must become an octopus.

Thoroughly knowing the political and regulatory environment in which you operate is one of the aspects your tentacles must master. It is of paramount importance to make the right decisions.

Here are a few of the subjects that need your attention:
- Consider what the social climate is like. Assess the strength of unions in your country and establish whether your workers are sufficiently or excessively protected.
- Always know the cost of layoffs.
- Investigate the rules for restructuring.
- Assess the strength of your country's environmental regulations. They might be becoming more stringent, in which case calculate how much you will need to invest to keep up in the coming years.
- Think about the fiscal administration to which you are subject. Are they on a witch-hunt or will they give you breathing space?
- The authorities *could* be more lenient and understanding if you employ a lot of people. If not, they might just accelerate your downfall through stupid regulations and controls.
- Look at whether you're dependent on international trade. If so, keep a constant watch on how the landscape's evolving. Think, for example, about how much protectionism and isolationism you are facing.

- Make sure your know-how, trademarks and brands are sufficiently protected so no one can copy you.
- Know which certifications you need to sell your products. OEKO-TEX? ISO? Bluesign? DIN? Also know the cost of keeping them up to date.
- Find out whether you're registered as a risky business from an environmental or safety point of view. If you are, study the regulations you need to abide by.

SUBSIDIES

As a liberal economics enthusiast, I don't believe that any company should rely on artificial money (subsidies) to survive. And everybody is abusing the system, which I loathe. However, if you have a bright cookie in your team who has the time and mindset to pitch for subsidies, they should certainly do so. But *never* be dependent on this money. Subsidies will not save your ass.

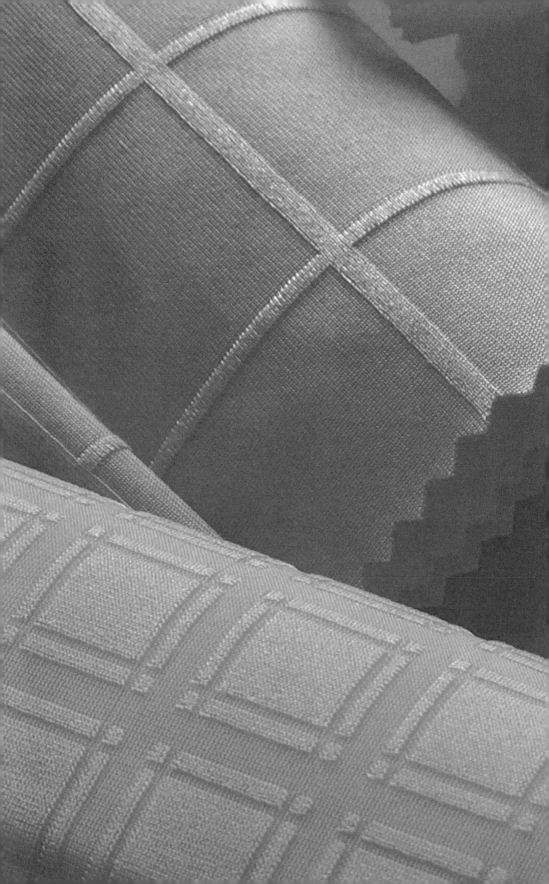

CONCLUSION

There is not one conclusion to this book, and nor should there be. Business is not an exact science. There is no opening, middle game and endgame – no unequivocal proof to be delivered. Every input leads to a different output. There are too many moving parts, both literally and figuratively. It's what makes business interesting and worthwhile – but also insidious, stressful and consuming. It is a game of emotions, and an infinite game at that.

Throughout my journey, I have found that business is a sport in its own way. A tightrope walk between the temptations of life. A never-ending battle to find the golden mean. There is *hubris* lurking on the left and *vanitas* on the right – we must always be wary of the arrogance of Icarus and the vanity of Nero. This is a tantalizing torment in a world where growth, profit and success beat the drum. And it's up to the CEO to keep the rhythm – to find that sweet spot of peace and balance. Despite the mountains of business manuals and the sea of information, there is no single solution; no ready-made, copy-paste solution to your problem; no 'verified guide' on how to be a fair boss and a good partner; no warning signs of your troubles. Just you, your team and your business. And a lot of trial and error. It is an unforgiving game.

This book is not a little red book with quotations from a chairperson. At best, this book serves as a compilation of practical and hard-won advice for managers and owners of any company in a situation similar to mine. I titled it *Mastering Decline* to capture a decades-long odyssey through the business world and a few lessons learned. It is the kind of book I wish I'd had when I was 28 years old, when I lost my role model, my best friend, and the CEO of our family and business – when I was forced to make a decision I never thought I'd have to make at that age.

With the benefit of hindsight, this book could easily have been called *Mastering Life*, since business is inextricably linked with life. It's unusual but not illogical to think of businesspeople as athletes, competing at the top of their game. This is a concept I embraced long ago and put into practice: a CEO should adopt the lifestyle of an athlete – go to sleep at a reasonable hour, adopt a healthy work–life balance, value their personal time, master their game and have fun! There are many dos and even more don'ts. But it takes strong willpower and unwavering dedication to keep walking the tightrope of life and not to be overconfident or vain. Because the highs are high, but the lows are lower. Luckily, in business as in life, I have been surrounded by the best and the brightest – an A-list of intelligent, motivated and loyal individuals who have kept me in check when I needed it most. This is perhaps the most important key takeaway of this book: choose your partners wisely. This is an absolute *conditio sine qua non*. And, frankly, it is also the one that I've had the most luck with, as I've chosen the best life partner any man could ever wish for.

Albert Einstein is widely quoted as once having written to his son, "Life is like riding a bicycle. To keep your balance, you must keep moving."

That is what the story of Icarus tells us. And it's also what 30 years in business have taught me: find the right balance, be prepared, take decisions and move forward. Don't trust the motion of the ocean but take control of the ship. I have been fortunate enough to navigate our ship in troubled waters, to balance our books in a declining market.

A close-knit team: the Liebaert family in action in Costa Rica, 2008.

Sometimes we just hit a stroke of good fortune, but most of the time that 'fortune' results from endless hours of preparation, a healthy sense of intuition and a clear view of where the company is headed. And, of course, a lot of guts to make tough decisions when shit hits the fan.

'Decline' is usually defined as 'sinking to a lower level' or, figuratively, as 'falling to an inferior or impaired condition.' In a way, the title of this book is misleading. Of course, Liebaert Textiles is no longer what it used to be. But, given the market circumstances, its earlier form was no longer justified. The exodus of many competitors to Asia had left Liebaert against the ropes. But then we remembered the story of the lily and the lion. We Liebaerts have never been fond of rules and 'must dos.' Rather than yielding to expectations, Liebaert chose to fight back and master the decline. However, that doesn't mean that we've sunk to a lower level. On the contrary even, decline has taught us to evolve to a whole new level, where steeper margins, immeasurable profit and exuberant growth have been traded for corporate efficiency, quality innovation and actual sustainability. We've adapted ourselves to the market. And hopefully, one day, the market will adapt to us. Only then will I be able to truly claim that we've mastered decline.

GLOSSARY

40-gauge weftlock	The finest weftlock machine in the world.
Beam dyeing	A piece-dyeing process whereby the fabric is wound on a perforated beam and then dyed in a closed high-pressure vessel.
Carbon fibre knitting	Carbon fibres break once they are bent and are therefore almost impossible to knit. For the moment, they are only used in weaving and multi-axial production (laying fibres on top of each other to produce big 'mattresses' of fibres that are then impregnated with resins) used in the production of blades for windmills and hulls of ships. We made several trials to produce knitted carbon fibres and succeeded in making samples but had no success in the market.
Continuous dyeing or pad-steam dyeing	A fabric dyeing process whereby the fabric is dyed and washed in a continuous flow. Our elastic tapes are dyed using this process.

Digital printing A fabric printing process whereby a fabric is printed using printing nozzles filled with ink, comparable to inkjet printers for paper printing.

Gauge A unit that measures the fineness of a knitting machine in number of needles per inch.

Gore-Tex™ A membrane added on a fabric as a water repellent and moisture management tool.

Jet dyeing A discontinuous fabric dyeing process in which the fabric circulates freely through the dye bath. All our fabrics are dyed using one of these processes (beam dyeing or jet dyeing).

Lycra™ Elastane or polyurethane elastic fibre used in conjunction with a hard fibre (nylon, polyester or cotton) to produce elastic fabrics and narrows.

Micro threads A yarn consisting of different filaments of less than one decitex. (One decitex: one gram per 10,000 metres of yarn).

Nanostitch™ Special fabrics made by Liebaert on the finest warp knitting machine in the world with 50 needles per inch.

Narrow weaving A weaving process that uses special needle looms which are equipped to produce elastic tapes, as we produce at Liebaert.

Needle righting A warp knitting machine often has over 5,000 needles next to each other. If the space between the needles is not perfect within a tenth of a millimetre, the fabric will be striped and discarded. Specially skilled people need to make sure that all the needles are perfectly centred ('righted'), which is a very difficult and exhausting job. We succeeded in automizing part of this job.

Recto Verso™ Liebaert's brand of athleisure.

Recto Verso Elite™ Liebaert's brand of compression garments for elite athletes.

Rotary printing A fabric printing process whereby the fabric passes over a set of cylinders filled with coloured paste each representing a different colour.

Second choice fabrics Fabrics that do not reach our expected quality criteria and are discarded.

Warp knitting A knitting technology whereby the yarns are knitted in the length direction.

Weft knitting or circular knitting   A knitting technology whereby the yarns are knitted in the width direction (or circular). Socks, panties and most T-shirts are knitted in this way.

Weftlock   A unique warp knitting machine knitting an elastane yarn, both in warp as in weft direction. The very high Lycra content gives a unique compression to the fabric.